Reading In-Between

Reading In-Between

How Minoritized Cultural Communities
Interpret the Bible in Canada

EDITED BY

Néstor Medina
Alison Hari-Singh
HyeRan Kim-Cragg

PICKWICK *Publications* · Eugene, Oregon

READING IN-BETWEEN
How Minoritized Cultural Communities Interpret the Bible in Canada

Pickwick Publications
An Imprint of Wipf and Stock Publishers
199 W. 8th Ave., Suite 3
Eugene, OR 97401

www.wipfandstock.com

PAPERBACK ISBN: 978-1-5326-4182-4
HARDCOVER ISBN: 978-1-5326-7485-3
EBOOK ISBN: 978-1-7252-5055-0

Cataloguing-in-Publication data:

Names: Medina, Néstor, editor. | Hari-Singh, Alison, editor. | Kim-Cragg, HyeRan, editor.

Title: Reading in-between : how minoritized cultural communities interpret the Bible in Canada / edited by Néstor Medina, Alison Hari-Singh, and HyeRan Kim-Cragg.

Description: Eugene, OR: Pickwick Publications, 2019. | Includes bibliographical references.

Identifiers: ISBN 978-1-5326-4182-4 (paperback). | ISBN 978-1-5326-7485-3 (hardcover). | ISBN 978-1-7252-5055-0 (ebook).

Subjects: LCSH: Bible—Hermeneutics—Cross-cultural studies. | Bible—Canada. | Bible—Criticism, interpretation, etc.

Classification: BS476 R36 2019 (print). | BS476 (ebook).

Manufactured in the U.S.A.   02/14/19

Contents

Contributors

Catherine Aldred is a member of the Metis Nation of British Columbia and a self-identifying Plains Cree. She received her MA in Religious and Translation studies with specialization in First Nations languages from McGill University. Catherine is a translation coordinator with Canadian Bible Society. She currently lives in her hometown, Grande Prairie, Alberta, Canada.

Raymond Aldred (ThD [ABD] Wycliffe College, University of Toronto) is status Cree from Swan River Band, Treaty 8. Born in Northern Alberta, he now resides with his wife in Richmond, British Columbia, Canada. Ray is the director of the Indigenous Studies Program at the Vancouver School of Theology whose mission is to partner with the Indigenous Church around Indigenous Identity and theological education. He is also an ordained minister of the Christian and Missionary Alliance in Canada.

Alison Hari-Singh (PhD [ABD] Wycliffe College, University of Toronto) is Administrator of the Doctor of Ministry Program at the Toronto School of Theology, on the campus of the University of Toronto. She was born in London, U.K., and immigrated to a small town in northern Saskatchewan with her family when she was a child. She holds a B.Sc. (Hons.) in Psychology from the University of Toronto and an M.Rel. from Wycliffe College. She is ordained in the Anglican Church of Canada and has been appointed Assistant Curate of the Church of St. Martin in-the-Fields, Toronto.

HyeRan Kim-Cragg (PhD Emmanuel College, University of Toronto) is Lydia Gruchy Professor of Pastoral Studies at St. Andrew's College, Saskatoon, Canada. She is the author of *Story and Song* (Peter Lang, 2012), *Interdependence* (Pickwick, 2018) and coauthor with Mary Ann Beavis of *Hebrews* (Liturgical Press, 2015) and *What Does the Bible Say?* (Cascade, 2017). Her research interests range from preaching, postcolonial studies, migration, anti-racism education, ecological justice, feminist liturgy, pastoral leadership, to intercultural and interreligious practices and ministries.

Barbara M. Leung Lai (PhD University of Sheffield) is research Professor of Old Testament at Tyndale University College & Seminary, Toronto, Canada. Dr. Leung Lai has published widely in peer-reviewed journals, chapters in academic books & Festschrifts, articles in Study Bibles and dictionary entries. She is the author of *Proverbs* (DienDao, 2004); *Through the "I"-Window: The Inner Life of Characters in the Hebrew Bible* (Sheffield Phoenix, 2011); *and Glimpsing the Mystery: The Book of Daniel* (Lexham, 2016).

Alan Ka Lun Lai (EdD Columbia University) was born and raised in Hong Kong. He came to Canada to pursue university education. He has taught at Wilfrid Laurier University and Vancouver School of Theology, specializing in educational ministries, Asian Christianity in North America, and Jewish-Christian relations. Alan is ordained in the Lutheran tradition and ministers at Richmond Chinese United Church in Vancouver.

Néstor Medina (PhD St. Michael's College, University of Toronto) is a Visiting Scholar at the Emmanuel College Centre for Religion and its Context. A recipient of the Louisville Book Grant for Minority Scholars (2014–15) and Research Grant (2018). He is the author of *Mestizaje* (Orbis, 2009), which was the winner of the 2012 Hispanic Theological Initiative's Book Award; *On the Doctrine of Discovery* (CCC, 2017), and *Christianity, Empire, and the Spirit* (Brill, 2018). He studies the intersection between people's cultures, histories, ethnoracial relations, forms of knowledge and religious/theological traditions.

Greer Anne Wenh-In Ng (PhD Columbia University) is an Associate Professor Emerita at Emmanuel College, Victoria University in the University of Toronto. Previously she also taught at the Vancouver School of Theology and Trinity Theological College, Singapore. She is an ordained minister of The United Church of Canada and has served her denomination locally, regionally, and nationally. Wenh-In currently co-chairs Emmanuel College's Committee on Asian/North American Asian Theologies.

Gosnell L. Yorke (PhD in Biblical Studies, McGill University, 1987) is an AfriCanadian. In addition, he studied for two years at the McGill Law School (1986–1988). Currently, he teaches in, and coordinates the PhD program for the Dag Hammarskjöld Institute for Peace and Conflict Studies at The Copperbelt University, Zambia. As a trained Bible Translation Consultant who has worked for the United Bible Societies in the Africa Region (1996–2006) and a member of SNTS (since 2001), Yorke has also published extensively in the areas of biblical studies, and Bible translation and language use in Africa and its diaspora.

1

Introduction

THIS PROJECT HAS BEEN long in the making. The idea began with "Minority Biblical Interpretation in Canada," a panel organized by Fernando Segovia as part of the Bible in Racial, Ethnic, and Indigenous Communities Group of the American Academy of Religion held in 2009 in Montreal. The panel drew together younger scholars from racialized backgrounds to discuss how they read the Bible as immigrants and visible minoritized groups in Canada. Afro-Caribbean, East Asian, South Asian, and Latino voices were all represented as they spoke to a mainly white, Canadian audience. The room was buzzing, filled with energy that comes when something important and potentially ground-breaking is about to happen. After returning home from Montreal, Néstor and Alison began talking about compiling the presentations. It soon became clear, however, that a greater focus was needed than what had been discussed at the panel session. Néstor and Alison were curious about whether immigrants who are ethnically minoritized Christians in the theological academy could identify and name a biblical hermeneutic or way of reading the Bible from within their own ethno-cultural community. The idea was to step away consciously from standard Euro-North American methodologies for reading the Bible, and to draw, instead, from our own communities to present ways of reading the biblical text that are equally legitimate to the normative approaches taught in seminaries and schools of theology in Canada.

Ultimately, the goal was to bring together a set of high quality articles wrestling with the question of how our ethno-culturally minoritized communities engage the biblical narrative within a Canadian context. These contributions were not to be exegetical papers or explorations and adaptations of other biblical approaches (e.g., liberationist, postcolonial, historico-critical, etc.), although there may have been connections and parallels. Moreover, the papers were not to be a mere theoretical exercise as, for example, Fernando Segovia's own *Decolonizing Biblical Studies*. What Néstor and Alison wanted was for the contributors to produce papers that took their own ethnocultural background and tradition seriously. It is for this reason that they chose the title *Reading in-Between*, acknowledging how different ethno-cultural communities negotiate and navigate the spaces between their particular cultural traditions and the reading of the biblical text. Néstor and Alison wanted the contributors to this project to make explicit the ways in which their ethnocultural community approaches the biblical text and how this reflected the narratival hermeneutic we were seeking in this collection.

Both Néstor and Alison felt this quest was vitally important to be asked in a Canadian context. They realized it was not that difficult to find this kind of reading within African American, Latina/o, Asian, and Native American Indigenous communities in the USA.[1] In Canada, however, this type of reflection has not been documented. Considering the emphasis on multicultural-ism in Canada, this seemed like a significant lacuna in the aca-demic and pastoral literature. The Canadian context is unique and peoples from different ethnocultural traditions—including recent immigrants to this country—have specific concerns. Thus, the literature addressing such concerns within the context of the USA is unsuitable and insufficient.

The realization of this project has been more difficult to fulfill than either Néstor or Alison were expecting. Not only did many of our participants back out, but they did so often because the question we were asking them took more time to consider

---

1. See, for example, Bailey et al., eds., *They Were All in One Place*.

than they were able to give. Every one of our contributors—those whose papers are included in this collection and those whose papers were withdrawn by the authors themselves—has many other responsibilities within their communities. This fact points to some of the systemic issues faced by immigrant communities to provide not only for their immediate families, but their extended families (that is, their communities) as well. Their multiple located identities, which come with multiple loyalties and responsibilities, were apparent in the arduous journey giving birth to this volume. It is easy in certain ethnocultural communities to become overburdened, especially as pastors, academics, and leaders. The other difficulty we faced was that some of the people we asked to contribute simply found the question too difficult to answer. For those of us from minoritized backgrounds, the sway of the dominant Euro-Canadian culture of the North Atlantic often places a set of blinders on us that dampen our ability to reflect theologically from our own ethnocultural vantage point. Approaching the biblical narrative, therefore, as what we are—racialized, marginalized, and immigrant Christians in the Canadian context—is thwarted. We have been subtly (and not so subtly) taught to de-legitimate our own experiences as perspectival (read as insufficient), emotional, illogical, and more likely to be in error. Yet the approaches to reading Scripture that dominate the North Atlantic are equally perspectival (read as value laden), responding to specific Eurocentric concerns, and potentially erroneous. Thus, the task set before each contributor was at times frustrating and difficult. The question had seldom, if ever, been considered before, and many were not able to complete the task.

In an effort not to let this important project slip away due to the constraints already named, Néstor enlisted the help of HyeRan Kim-Cragg. HyeRan provided the project a renewed sense of energy and a passionate voice. The three of us worked together to find new contributors who were willing to take on the challenge of this task.

The upshot, this volume is comprised of three sections: an introduction, six essays and two responses. The six essays are arranged in two sections. The first section includes three essays from our contributors of East Asian descent: Alan Lai, Barbara Leung Lai, and HyeRan Kim-Cragg. Grouping the papers in this way was not intentional, but proved significant to the shape of the book in the end. These first three papers present a more intentional engagement with the biblical text itself. Using concrete examples, they each demonstrate how one's ethnocultural experiences and current social location converge to produce a reading that is quite unlike what we have inherited from dominant Euro-North American biblical hermeneutics. The second section is more methodological in content and intention. Néstor Medina, Alison Hari-Singh, and Ray Aldred each challenge readers to rethink the nature of biblical hermeneutics. All three essays use story in completely different ways to get at the heart of how our respective communities go about reading the Bible. The third and final section includes two responses to these six essays. The first response is from Asian Canadian theologian and professor emeritus at Emmanuel College in Toronto, Wenh-In Ng, and the second is from Caribbean Canadian biblical scholar, Gosnell Yorke, who teaches at Copperbelt University in Zambia.

Among these unique, powerful, and thoughtful essays, however, there is a deficiency: the absence of Afro-Canadian voices in their diversity. This is a problem that we as editors fought hard to overcome. It has proven more difficult than we could have imagined. Despite this shortfall, we carried on with the project because the objective was, and continues to be, presenting a sample of the rich array of cultural voices within the Canadian landscape. Until the publication of this volume, these have been excluded from mainstream biblical hermeneutics. That said, in the months and years to come, as culturally located biblical hermeneutics are discussed more widely in our churches and within the theological academy in Canada, it is our sincere hope that Black voices—and others that are absent—will be added to those found here. The limit of this volume, paradoxically, speaks to the urgent need to develop more work like this one. This volume can be understood as a modest stepping-stone for other ethnoculturally minoritized

Christian Canadians to step out, make their voices heard, and offer their wisdom to the larger Christian church.

Furthermore, what might come as a surprise is that this entire experience has been a lesson in intercultural relations for us as co-editors of this volume. We have endeavored to allow the voices of our contributors simply to speak without ourselves—editors with our own specific cultural interests—getting in the way. What you have in the pages before you are journeys—ones you probably would not have encountered otherwise. We hope that in reading this volume, the biblical story comes alive to you in new and fresh ways as you consider your own context and how each of us brings a perspectival approach to reading the most formative book of the church and our lives.

Alan Lai's paper looks at the influence of Confucianism on how Chinese immigrants read and understand the Bible in Canada today. He observes that one of Confucianism's greatest tenets is that "heaven and earth are one." This means that in order to follow "the way" and understand "the great ultimate," one must be educated. Education is not simply book learning, but rather learning how to be human and humane. This takes intellectual effort and behavioral change. One must work at perfectibility. In light of this, it is not surprising that attraction to Christian pietism followed missionary efforts in China. Many Chinese Christians today are evangelical Protestants for whom pious personal conduct in conformity with tradition, absolute values, certainty, and spiritual growth is emphasized. In this way, Chinese evangelical churches find affinity and resonate with Confucian thought. Likewise, Confucian thought influences how Chinese evangelicals read the Bible. Morality, personal faith, and individual integrity are significant lenses that define a *Confucian reading* of the Bible in Chinese evangelical churches. A drawback, however, is the lack of emphasis on those biblical texts that are concerned with social justice. These are overlooked as being too political. A younger generation of Chinese Christians may be challenging this Confucian influence, however. The younger generation, according to Lai, longs for more openness, inclusivity, and social change. The upshot for Chinese

Christians in Canada is that Confucian values and Christianity are not antithetical. Both tenets can be and are accommodated within the lives of Chinese Canadian Christians.

Barbara Leung Lai's paper explores how her Chinese heritage and Canadian situatedness affects her reading of Ecclesiastes. Over the last two decades, her methodological approach has moved toward a more experiential, perspectival, and narratival approach to reading Wisdom literature. In this essay, Leung Lai documents a Chinese Canadian reading of Ecclesiastes and the significance this holds for Chinese Canadian readers. She is also concerned with how this culturally specific reading of Ecclesiastes might generate a paradigm for living well as a Christian person of any cultural background. Leung Lai's approach is to examine three important concepts: (1) the Chinese notion of self or selfhood, (2) the idea of meaninglessness or emptiness in the Chinese psyche, and (3) the cultural value of perseverance in Chinese philosophy. Finally, Leung Lai looks at how these three characteristics influence the collective lived experiences of diasporic Chinese immigrants in Canada when it comes to reading Ecclesiastes.

According to Leung Lai, self in Chinese culture is never an interior, autonomous, experiential existence; rather, the idea of "self" is "inextricably in dialogue with others." Just as our personal experiences are not divorced from the collective, neither can our approach to reading the biblical text be isolated from the community. The interaction of the "small self" with the "grand narrative" is an important aspect of how Leung Lai reads Ecclesiastes as a Chinese person. Likewise, meaninglessness is not a philosophical concept in Chinese thought, but a consequence of lived experience. In a culture that values the communal self over the individual self, the experience of turning to the self is connected to an understanding of emptiness or meaninglessness. Chinese culture lauds the virtue of "eating bitterness." Likewise, Ecclesiastes nurtures the Chinese reader's capacity to endure suffering and cope with life's difficulties. Consequently, as Leung Lai writes, for Chinese people, "sustaining in tension" is more esteemed than that of "resolving tension." In this sense, Chinese readers have a better understanding of what Ecclesiastes is all about.

Leung Lai concludes by taking this culturally specific reading of Ecclesiastes and identifying a moral ontology that may be lived out by those beyond the Chinese community. She draws on an analogy of bonding wood that creates a durable and very strong form of usable plywood. Leung Lai challenges readers, thus, to read in a way that *crosses the grains*—that is, combining one's own culturally located reading with the Chinese emphasis on embracing the complexity, joys, and difficulties of life. In sketching this culturally located Chinese reading of Ecclesiastes, Leung Lai affirms an approach that all Christians may employ in order to experience life more fully.

For HyeRan Kim-Cragg, sitting crossed-legged is a fundamental, existential posture for Korean people. It is a way to truly hear others. As it pertains to reading the Bible, sitting cross-legged—a posture of humility and receptiveness while being grounded—permits the hearing of those voices that may interpret the biblical text in ways contrary to standard Euro-North American readings. Kim-Cragg emphasizes a biblical hermeneutic of *inter-positioning* by which she means the "intentional crossing of disciplines." This hermeneutic of inter-positioning posits a recapitulation of the relation of theology, the Bible, and empire through multiple lenses of race, sexuality, colonial experience, gender, culture, language, and religious expression. Her essay looks at the story of Jephthah's daughter—a text largely ignored in mainline Protestant denominations. For Kim-Cragg, this oversight is a not so subtle reinforcement of androcentrism and patriarchy. Her goal is to unsettle patriarchal interpretations of this text by highlighting Korean feminist ritual as a way of reorienting how this biblical text is read.

Reading this difficult text alongside a group of Korean women, Kim-Cragg shows an alternative reading—one very different from dominant Eurocentric and androcentric readings. For Kim-Cragg (and the women with whom she studied this text), the Korean cultural emphasis on mourning and resistance are key aspects in interpretation. The women with whom she read this story brought their own experiences of conflict and marginalization to the text. But, surprisingly, they sympathized with Jephthah. He himself was a possible victim of the system and not necessarily a mighty man of war. Kim-Cragg shows how these women were also sympathetic to the negative position of Jephthah's daughter and made a connection between her status as a virgin under the oppression of militarism and colonization. They saw connections between Jephthah's daughter and the "comfort women" abused by soldiers of all nations during the Second World War.

Repeatedly, Kim-Cragg notes that this group of Korean women understood this narrative differently from traditional Western feminist readings. For example, Jephthah's daughter's virginity was interpreted as an honor and not limited by patriarchy and the violence of war. These Korean feminist readers celebrated Jephthah's daughter as being able to wield authority in her own life. They understood the very telling of the story as a challenge to patriarchy and violence—that is, the sacrifice of women and children must come to an end. They heard the story as calling for the creation of a new narrative, one that embodies the restoration of the world. Moreover, these women also understood mourning as a communal ritual key to healing and sharing one's burdens. For these Korean women, mourning is an act of resistance. Together, they affirmed this story as not being simply for Jewish ears but also Korean communities and all women around the globe. Based on this encounter in a Korean women's bible study, Kim-Cragg's approach—inter-positioning—is ultimately a gesture of flexibility, negotiation, and resistance.

Néstor Medina looks at how different cultural communities—particularly those in the Latina/o community in Canada—situate themselves in the biblical narrative as well as how the traditions and stories of Latinas/os impact how the Bible is read and interpreted. Medina proposes that Latinas/os, even those who are from a more conservative, evangelical background, are not merely wedded to a "literalist" reading of the Bible but rather are in a dialogical relationship with the biblical text. In other words, Latinas/os lived-faith and lived experience is a hermeneutic unto itself—a *lived herme-neutics*. The everyday lives of Latina/o people inform how they read, understand, and interpret the Bible.

In terms of the Canadian context, the concrete existence of Latinas/os in Canada is that of recent immigrants. Alongside this identity comes experiences of discrimination, marginalization, and poverty. These lived-experiences impact how this community finds meaning in the biblical narrative. Medina indicates that there is an interweaving of the messiness of human life with reading the biblical text. Simultaneously, however, there is a great trust in the Scriptures. The narrative's emphasis on divine redemption (spiritu-ally, socio-politically, and economically) captivates Latinas/os. For them, the liberation found in the biblical text can be actualized in their own life circumstances today. The Bible is a word of hope— hope to address their new, often difficult, socio-political context as immigrants in Canada. It is this very experience of living in a diverse and multicultural Canada that challenges Latinas/os to move beyond the literalistic reading they may have acquired in their countries of origin or inherited from the traditions of which they are part. Furthermore, the experience of community also af-fects the lived hermeneutic of Latinas/os. Unlike many brought up in the traditions of the North Atlantic, autonomy is not overly emphasized in Latina/o communities. This means that reading the Bible is not merely for personal edification but also an act done within families and in the greater community—that is, those who share the Christian faith, those who've experienced marginaliza-tion in Canada, and those who have become "family." Thus, there is an axis of interaction between what the text means and how the reader lives that generates a concretized and lived hermeneutic. The upshot, Latina/o believers see themselves as being part of the biblical narrative. The biblical story is, in fact, their story. This is extremely liberating for those who are marginalized and discrimi-nated against on so many fronts.

Medina goes on to highlight how one can discern the bibli-cal hermeneutic of Latina/o Canadians. It is not through a kind of systematic theology as written dogmas, but in their songs, testimonies, preaching and prayers. That is, this lived hermeneutic can only be discerned by hearing an oral tradition. Orality is an epistemology—a way of knowing. This is connected closely to how the ancients of the Bible understood their traditions and heard their God. Therefore, orality should not be discredited out of hand. Within oral traditions, we find the "implicit theology" of a community and more "messy" interpretations of the biblical text. Songs, prayers, and testimonies speak of the dynamic interaction between the lived lives of Latinas/os, their encounter with the Bible, and the revelation of the divine within both their own lives and that of the narrative.

Alison Hari-Singh's essay aims to identify and name how South Asian Christians, particularly those from North India, approach reading the Bible. Based on her personal experiences with evangelical Christians from the Punjab, she names *Christian bhakti*—that is, utter devotion to and worship of God—as the approach by which many South Asian Christians living in Canada (and elsewhere in the diaspora) approach the biblical text. Hari-Singh examines this claim by discussing the archetypal life of a controversial twentieth-century North Indian Christian evangelist, mystic, and author named Sadhu Sundar Singh. Singh, a convert to Christianity, did not abandon an Indian way of thinking and knowing upon his conversion; rather, he integrated his experiences as a South Asian person with his life-altering encounter with Jesus Christ. Singh rejected the "English" way of worship into which he was baptized. Instead, he retained union with God, a Hindu concept, as the ultimate goal of Christian life. For Singh, union with God is the goal of any *bhakta* (practitioner of *bhakti*), whether Christian or Hindu. Furthermore, the way to experience this state of being is through devotional worship. This devotion, as it pertains to reading the biblical text, manifests in what Hari-Singh summarizes as three identifying markers: faith-filled reading, prayerful reading, and surrendered reading. For Hari-Singh, reflection on her experiences in South Asian Christian circles, hearing the Hindi Christian songs of her childhood, and watching how her parents and their friends ponder the Scriptures in an attitude of faith and trust—prayerfully and devoutly reading each word so that they may know God in fullness—is best described as *Christian bhakti*. *Bhakti*, a distinctly South Asian religious way of being, is the biblical hermeneutic by which many South Asian Christians from North India have read and continue to read the Bible in Canada.

Ray Aldred (writing with his daughter Catherine Aldred-Schull) has switched trajectories in his objective of reading the Bible. Instead of looking for propositional truth within the text, Aldred has begun to read the biblical text as story—which is what it means to read the biblical text as a Cree person. Aldred takes a step back from the initial intention of this volume toward a more primary concern within his community: translation. As with all of us contributing to this volume, Aldred would not have known the gospel story without the translation of the biblical text into our respective original languages. Thus, in order to make his point, Aldred outlines the history of Bible translation among Cree people in Canada.

Aldred rejects any method of interpretation that aims to "civilize" others, and currently, most translations of the Bible into Cree do not seek to express the gospel in what Aldred calls the "heart language" of Indigenous peoples. Thus, the translations that exist are a false representation of how the gospel is understood by First Nations, Métis, and Inuit communities. What is overlooked is that, at their core, Indigenous languages are primarily oral and performative in nature. The Bible, however, is no longer an oral tradition, but a written document, and, as Aldred puts it, "a Western construct." In order to be read well by Indigenous peoples, any translation of the Bible must emphasize story and be performed in community. The only way to do this, Aldred argues, is for the gospel to be told and heard in a way that conforms to the heart of the Good News—that is, a *hermeneutic of love*. Indigenous people themselves are the only ones who can do this type of work of translation effectively for their communities. First Nations, Métis, and Inuit people need to be able to converse on their own terms with the original languages of the Bible as well as their mother tongues.

Only then will the translation be faithful to the "heart language" of Indigenous peoples in Canada.

Ultimately, for Alfred, the key elements required for an appropriate translation of the Bible into Cree include attention to the communal character and dynamic mutuality of Indigenous identity (i.e., the value of the many over the one), and the narratival or story-based character of Indigenous cultures. Aldred reiterates that the oral nature of Indigenous cultures aids in biblical hermeneutics because Indigenous peoples already have a long-held understanding of "how story works." Furthermore, there must be an emphasis on humility as a primary characteristic of narratival memory and an acknowledgement that narratives are open-ended. Finally, and maybe most importantly, there needs to be an emphasis on location or place—the fourth world—rather than on time, because First Nations, Métis, and Inuit spiritualities are essentially connected to place and land.

None of these aspects named above have been part of the work of translating the Bible from English (notably not the original languages of the Bible) into Cree. Therefore, the biblical text with which Cree people have to work is not connected to Indigenous aspirations but rather a repetition of the insights and values of the Europeans who brought the Bible to them in the first place. For Alfred, a theology of Scripture that brings the ethnocultural location of Cree people to a reading of the text cannot truly begin until Cree people themselves can communicate the central core of their traditions and cultures while remaining faithful to the biblical text they have encountered and through which they have come to believe.

This book concludes with reflections from Chinese Canadian theologian Wenh-In Ng and Caribbean Canadian biblical scholar Gosnell Yorke, both of whom attended the original panel in Montreal almost 9 years ago. Ng begins her response to this volume by highlighting where the minoritized-Canadian readings of the Bible presented here may be located within the wider scope of scholarship—that is, vis-à-vis minoritized scholars writing from a USA context. She continues by making an exceptionally important clarification about the nature of the essays in this volume. These socio-culturally rooted narrative hermeneutics, she writes, are clearly written *by* minoritized scholars and *about* their respective minoritized communities, but the question remains as to whether they are *for* minoritized readers. Based on this initial assessment, Ng groups the essays into three categories, singling out the Indigenous contribution of Ray Aldred and Catherine Aldred-Schull as well as the Latino/a narratival hermeneutic offered by Néstor Medina while grouping the Asian-rooted offerings of Alan Lai, Barbara Leung Lai, HyeRan Kim-Cragg and Alison Hari-Singh together. She engages each contributor's essay through her own personal experience as a minoritized person who has long been occupied with this task in the Canadian context.

Consequently, Ng asks four important questions of this volume and its contributors: (1) When and where are minoritized Christians doing these readings? (2) Who is doing these readings and with whom? (3) Where do minoritized readers engage the Bible? and (4) How might minoritized Christians learn to read "*in-between*?" First, what Ng points out is that minoritized readers of the Bible are reading Scripture in a colonized context. Second, she notes that it is not only racialized academics, necessarily, who are engaging in narratival hermeneutics but also lay people from all walks of life. Third, lay folk are primarily engaging in these readings in their local churches and communities. Finally, Ng notes how global migration permits a level of interaction and mutuality with those unlike ourselves in ways that were previously inconceivable. Ng affirms that as racially and ethnically minoritized Christians, we must continue to do this work of reading in-between with "fear and trembling"—unlearning the stereotypes we have come to believe about cultures that are not ours in order to enliven our own perspective. Lastly, and most importantly, Ng observes that we must be aware of cultural appropriation. Until this awareness sets in and we truly begin to take each other at face value on the "other's" own terms, we will be hard-pressed not to oppress one another. What Ng offers here is not simply a summation of all the individual contributions to this volume or the moments of nexus that we all share as minoritized people; rather, she highlights the differences that remain between us and between the minoritized and the racially and ethnically dominant. This is a critical reminder and a helpful insightful.

Gosnell Yorke takes an alternate approach in terms of his assessment of this short collection of essays. Yorke situates his response in the legal, multi-cultural context of Canada, highlighting the official bilingual ideal of French and English that Canada claims to embody. It is in this context that minoritized and racialized Canadians read the Bible. Consequently, Yorke lauds this volume for giving voice to what he calls the "voiceless visibles." Yorke notes that the "narratival hermeneutics" expressed in this volume demonstrates the dialogical interplay between the individual and one's community of formation in a variety of ways. To separate the two is impossible, yet foundational and necessary to good biblical hermeneutics. This approach, however, is antithetical to the dominant, Euro-normative readings of the biblical text that have long held sway in Canada.

Yorke does not endeavor to summarize the papers. Instead, he brings them into conversation with his own ethno-cultural location as a Caribbean man who is a naturalized Canadian citizen, but now works and resides in Zambia. What is found in this contribution is a critique of the *sine qua non* essentialization of the characteristics and nature of each contributor's ethno-cultural location. Yorke draws connections between the roots of each tradition presented here and that of his own experience in the African diaspora: between South Asian non-dualism and the ways of thinking in Black slave society, between the East Asian understanding of the "I-text" in Ecclesiastes with the "I-stress" amongst Rastas in Jamaica, and between the dialectical narratival hermeneutics of evangelical Latinos/as rooted in a situatedness of hardship and the Afro-Christian community that experiences a similar dispossession (to highlight just a few). Yorke does not make these connections in order to negate the very real differences between all the contributors but rather to highlight and acknowledge the points of connection between us for the purposes of solidarity.

Ng's and Yorke's reflections on these essays, rooted in their own particular experiences, serve to enhance the breadth and diversity of this volume. As readers journey with all of the contributors and both respondents, we as editors expect that they will not only find a variety of culturally specific biblical hermeneutics but also the "first fruits" of various theologies of Scripture rooted in our respective and distinct experiences. Since Scripture is theological in nature, questions regarding its intent and purpose cannot help but come to the fore. This may be the most unintentionally significant aspect of this volume and one that needs further study. This volume questions a compartmentalization of the Bible and theology (as well as other disciplines) as if they exist as detached, unrelated fields of study. Instead, the contributions call for close attention to the intertwined nature of academic disciplines.

Ultimately, locating our reading of the Bible in our cultural experiences is not an attempt to deemphasize the importance of the biblical text, as some of our readers may presume, but rather to show just how living and active the Bible is in the midst of our communities. Each of the articles in this collection affirms our initial intuition and insight that one's ethnocultural background and tradition plays a central role in the way people approach, read, and interpret the biblical text. Naming these culturally specific methodologies is not for our personal edification. Rather, we hope that these recently identified hermeneutics may be gleaned by those inside and outside our communities such that when accessed and utilized, they may bear good fruit, shaping our churches into communities where the Word is boldly spoken, truly heard, and faithfully lived.

One final word: this volume would not be possible if it were not for each author making the commitment and then taking the time to write his or her piece. We honor the voices here and celebrate the diversity of the Christian church in Canada. A special thanks to "Emmanuel College's Centre for Religion and its Context" and its "Committee on Asian/North American Asian Theologies" (CANAAT). Their financial support made it possible for us to move this project to the publication stage. Finally, we are grateful to our partners: Samia Saad, Jeff Nowers, and David Kim-Cragg. Much of the time we dedicated to this volume was valuable time taken away from our own families. Their support has proven crucial in this journey.

Néstor Medina, Alison Hari-Singh, and HyeRan Kim-Cragg

2

Chinese Canadian Identities and the Reading of the Bible

Alan Ka Lun Lai

Who are Chinese Canadian Christians? What has shaped and continues to shape the ways they read the Bible? Chinese in Canada are not a homogeneous group nor do they possess a singular cultural identity. Similarly, the phrase *Chinese Canadian Christians* points to the enormous diversity of these people. The number of Christian theological traditions and theological viewpoints are staggering enough to prevent anyone from addressing them as if they were a monolithic entity. These people, Christians or not, have come to Canada from various parts of Asia at different times, while others were born in Canada. Chinese Canadians speak different Chinese dialects in addition to the official Canadian languages. A Chinese Vietnamese Canadian living in Quebec would feel at home speaking French, while other immigrants residing in other parts of the country may struggle with the English language. In the past, Chinese who left their ancestral homeland were regarded as *traitors* and have long been described by the generalized term *huaquio* ("overseas Chinese"). Once they left their homeland, they were no longer regarded as authentic Chinese when compared to those who stayed. In a similar fashion, upon arriving in Canada, Chinese were perceived as not being genuine Canadians by the dominant

Euro-white Canadians. These dynamics shape the way Chinese Christian Canadians read and interpret the Bible.

In the following, I am interested in exploring the cultural dimension of the ways these diverse communities of Chinese Christian Canadians read the biblical text. I am not necessarily explaining the hermeneutics as developed by Chinese Christians in Euro-North America. Rather, I wish to outline the factors that may have shaped their approach to reading the Bible. I also wish to explore how the search for identity and the dynamics of uprooting and re-settlement in the complex Canadian sociocultural world impact such readings of the Bible. I suggest that the cultural characteristic of Confucian piety and the challenge of adaptation in Canada play significant roles in influencing the way many Chinese interpret the biblical text.

Who Are Chinese Canadians?

Chinese started coming to Canada around the mid-nineteenth century. They came as cheap laborers to build the Canadian Pacific Railway and work in the mines. Others also came to search for gold in the Fraser Valley in British Columbia. These Chinese lived in small ghettoes in Victoria, British Columbia and Toronto, Ontario, and were scattered somewhere in between. These laborers usually came from the lower strata of Chinese society in southern China and often with no knowledge of English at all. Sometimes, these people were called *sojourners*,[1] because they did not intend to settle in Canada; they came with a dream of returning home rich.[2] Their dreams were seldom realized. Their financial situations were so precarious that most of them ended up staying as permanent residents. Chinese Canadian poet Wayson Choy's best seller books *The Jade Peony* and *Paper Shadows: A Chinatown Childhood* provide excellent fictional portrayals of the social worlds of early Chinese workers, who were mostly single men. They confined

1. Yang, "Sojourners or Settlers," 61.
2. Yang, *Chinese Christians*, 29.

themselves in Chinatown, followed various Chinese religious practices, and formed social associations.

After the railroad was completed, these Chinese sojourners opened restaurants, laundries, and developed vegetable farms. The Canadian economy was stagnant in the early twentieth century. Since Chinese labourers would accept lower wage for menial tasks, they were seen as competitors in the struggling job market by local Euro-Canadians. Agitation against Chinese laborers became severe.[3] In addition, utilitarian attitudes among industrialists depicted Chinese as useful labourers but undesirable citizens. From 1884 to 1923, the British Columbia legislature passed numerous bills restricting the political and social rights of Chinese.[4] Racist names such as *Chinamen* and *Steam Engine* were imposed onto these settlers. In 1885, the Canadian government passed laws to disenfranchise Chinese in the form of a head tax. In 1923, the Canadian Immigration Act was passed to prevent all Asians from entering Canada. This Act was not repealed until 1947.[5]

Missionary efforts to convert Chinese by local churches were not particularly successful during this period. Churches functioned more as community centers for new immigrants. They were places where English language classes were held for adults and cultural heritage classes were provided for children. Social services were accessed through the churches.[6]

A second wave of Asian immigration began in 1965, when Canada amended their immigration laws. While immigration acts were repealed right after World War II, it would not be until 1965 when a further amendment to immigration laws allowed expanded influx of family members and relatives.[7] Most of these Chinese immigrants at this time were skilled workers or students in their prime working years—between the age of 15 and 34—and many of them intended to stay as permanent residents. Some immigrants

3. Li, *Chinese in Canada*, 24.
4. Li, *Chinese in Canada*, 32.
5. Li, *Chinese in Canada*, 89.
6. Yang, *Chinese Christians*, 38.
7. Li, *Chinese in Canada*, 93.

were family members of earlier immigrants. This was also the period when the Civil Rights movement in the United States of America and Europe began to take shape. Because of the influx of first-generation immigrants, the issues of inter-generational gaps and Chinese identities became important concerns.[8]

A third wave of Asian immigration occurred from 1985 onward, and this time they came as a entrepreneurs and investors. Most of these Chinese immigrants were Chinese from Hong Kong, but some also came from Taiwan and Singapore. Chinese immigrants in this period were mostly well-educated and cosmopolitan people who had substantial amounts of capital. As professionals and skilled workers, they were able to establish themselves in middle-class neighbourhoods and the suburbs. Chinatown became a place of commerce and a site for tourists; it had less significance for the daily life of these new immigrants. As they built Chinese infrastructure in suburbs, the significance of Chinatown for these professionals diminished. The uncertainty caused by the fear of China's communism caused many Chinese from Hong Kong to migrate to Western countries in the years leading up to 1997, when British-held Hong Kong was to be handed over to Mainland China. An estimated 260,000 Hong Kong residents migrated to Canada between 1980 and 1989.[9]

The end of the twentieth century marks an economic boom in Asia. Many Hong Kong Chinese were able to establish themselves in the wealthy, middle-class strata of Canadian society. In Vancouver, BC, the term "monster houses" refers to the phenomenon of Asian immigrants building mansion-style homes in prestigious neighborhoods that were not in harmony with traditional Canadian-style houses of the area. In the late 1990s, in Vancouver, there was a general perception that the wealthy Hong Kong buyers were the chief cause of skyrocketing real estate prices and a radical change in the architecture of houses.[10] Sociologist Peter Li argues that "the 'monster houses' controversy illustrates how a negative

8. Ng, "Pacific-Asian North American," 195.

9. Lai et al., "Chinese in Canada," 89–90.

10. Li, *Chinese in Canada*, 148.

racial image of the Chinese was socially constructed in the contemporary context, and how the Chinese were being stigmatized as wealthy foreigners who had little regard for the aesthetic values and traditional life-style of Canada."[11] The massive influx of well-to-do Chinese immigrants in this period created another wave of anti-Asian sentiments. It seems as if a similar situation is currently developing as contemporary housing markets in Vancouver and Toronto are skyrocketing; except this time, the anti-Asian sentiments are directed at Mainland Chinese buyers.

For the past ten years or more, with the economic boom of Mainland China, a significant number of Chinese from China has resettled in Canada. Traditionally, under the rule of the Communist Party, Mainland Chinese were said to be non-religious. While many Chinese are in fact non-religious, Christianity in China is growing rapidly. For the past few years, Christianity in China has been one of the fastest growing religions. It is particularly the case among the younger generation of Chinese. What makes Christianity attractive to Chinese young people is still a puzzling question. One may speculate that because of the country's constant contact with the West—due to its open door economic policy—Western culture and lifestyle are becoming increasingly popular. Many young people now find it fashionable to become Christians, a way to express their attraction to Western culture.[12]

Then, there are second, third, and fourth generation Chinese Canadians. These are the children of immigrants from various part of Asia. The term "1.5 generation" is used to denote those who were born in Asia but came to Canada at a relatively young age. These people are often called *bridge-persons* within the community as they well understand the culture and language of two worlds. Some, however, might contest describing the culture of these local born Chinese Canadians as Confucian—or to even call them Chinese—since many of them do not see themselves as Chinese but rather simply as Canadians.

11. Li, *Chinese in Canada*, 149.

12. Kaiser, "Church Growth in China," 46.

Chinese Cultures, Confucianism, and the Bible

Chinese came to know Christianity through Western missionaries. Before the eighteenth century, little was known about Christian activity in Asia.[13] Besides the Nestorians, who had successfully made their way to China in the eighth century, the most intensive interaction between the East and the West was led by the Jesuit missionaries of the seventeenth century. In China, these Roman Catholic priests engaged in serious dialogue with the Confucian scholars and they invested much of their time in studying Asian philosophy—notably, Confucianism.[14] The Jesuits praised Confucian institutions as well as Confucian philosophy. Matteo Ricci, for example, took Confucian studies very seriously, and he attempted to summarize Confucianism into an intellectual language that his friends back home in Portugal and Italy could understand.

The great missionary enterprise in China was the result of the Opium War (1839–1842).[15] Although not all Western missionaries were uncritical of the aggressive political and economic maneuvers of their home countries, the fact that they could enter China with guaranteed protection and freedom to preach Christianity shows they were not exempted from the accusation of imperialism.[16] After the Chinese lost the War, China was forced to sign the Treaty of Nanjing (1842). The result was that Hong Kong Island was conceded to the British and China was forced to open five coastal ports for trade.

The difference in approach by the Jesuits of the seventeenth century and Protestant missionaries of the nineteenth century

13. Depending on how one defines the term "Asia," Christian missionaries might have reached Asia very early in history. In Samuel Hugh Moffett's momentous work on the history of Christianity in Asia, Moffett discusses the presence of Christianity in Greco-Roman Asia, Iranian (Persian Asia), Indian Asia and Sinic (Chinese Asia). See Moffett, *History of Christianity in Asia*.

14. Spence, "Matteo Ricci," 13–15.

15. Before the Opium Wars, there were Western missionaries already working in China. The first Protestant Missionary in modern China was Robert Morrison of the London Missionary Society. Morrison arrived in Canton in September 1807. See Latourette, *History of Chinese Missions*, 211–12.

16. Lodwick, *Crusaders against Opium*, 30–41, 52, 129.

have been much debated. Jesuit missionaries expressed interest in Confucian and Chinese indigenous cultures. Although their presence in Asia was not without criticism, the Jesuits were more culturally sensitive to the host cultures. Unlike the Nestorians and the Jesuits of the former centuries, Western and Euro-North American missionaries of the nineteenth century forced their entry into China. Many of these were dedicated and sincere Christians perceiving that they had a better civilization, a better culture, and a God-given religion.[17]

The missionary enterprise in China was both a blessing and a curse.[18] The blessing included the opportunity to share the gospel with Chinese, providing medical services, building orphanages, and liberal education for women. It is undoubtedly true that Christian missionaries expanded the scope of education.[19] Yet, the availability for such an opportunity was forced-open by imperialistic military powers and interests. In retrospect, Western and Euro-North American missionaries functioned both as agents of Christianity and as agents of Western civilization. This fact instilled the perception in the Chinese that Christianity is a Western religion or, as the late Joseph Kitagawa put it, the *spiritual engine* of Western civilization, despite years of effort for indigenization.[20]

Archie Lee, a retired professor at Chung Chi College in the Chinese University of Hong Kong, makes an interesting observation concerning how the Bible may have been perceived in China.[21] He compares how the legendary and fictional classics of *Journey to the West* and the Bible made their way into Chinese societies. *The Journey to the West* portrays the extraordinary effort of the Buddhist monk Xuan Zang when he went to India on a quest for the precious Buddhist scriptures. He and his three disciples risked all kinds of danger *en route*. The story paints a vivid psychological

17. Chao, "Gospel and Culture," 15.

18. Vikner, "Lessons from the Church in China," 371.

19. Committee of Reference and Counsel, *Christian Education in China*, 256.

20. Kitagawa, *Christian Tradition*, 58.

21. Lee, "Bible in Chinese Christianity," 96–106.

picture whereby hard work is needed to obtain the precious Buddhist scriptures. This fictional work has been reproduced in countless television series. Its impact on the Chinese mind cannot be denied. The Bible, on the other hand, came from the West, brought by missionaries in the time of the Western colonial era. Unlike the Buddhist scriptures, as portrayed in the *Journey to the West*, the Western Bible forced its way into China without Chinese request and without much effort. Would this be one of the significant factors to explain why Chinese still find it difficult to claim the Bible as their own, that the Bible is still perceived as *non-Chinese*?

In order to help Chinese understand the Bible and to accept Christianity, many efforts have been made in translating the Bible and missionaries have spent great effort to explain why accepting the Christian faith is good for Chinese. In essence, the Bible is a Jewish document, but how Chinese Christians understand when they read the Bible and engage in a cross-cultural experience is unknown. It is clear, however, that Western missionaries taught Chinese to believe that the Bible is superior to other religious scripture and that the God portrayed in the Bible is the only one in whom it is worth believing. It is generally observed that Chinese churches tend to be either conservative or Evangelical. Korean theologian David Chung argues that there is much congeniality between Evangelicalism and Confucianism:

> We believed that a highly selective process took place in the minds especially of those who were inclined to accept Christianity when they were exposed to the Christian challenges. We also believe that the crystallized picture through this selective process was composed mainly of congenial elements."[22]

Confucianism is a way of life that is concerned with how people live harmoniously at home and in society. The basic Confucian affirmation is that heaven and earth are one. Confucian sages called it *The Great Ultimate*. Learning is crucial for one to follow *The Way*. In Chinese thought, education is not about book learning;

---

22. Chung, *Syncretism*, 107.

rather, it is about how to be human. It entails proper socially accepted conduct and behaviors. For those who have reached the stage of sagehood, learning is particularly important—not because they are endowed from above but rather because they have been true to their humanity.[23]

The overarching concern of Confucianism is the cultivation of self toward sainthood. Its main concern is self-cultivation.[24] It is true that personal moral cultivation should bring benefit to the social realm, yet the perfecting of self rather than society is the heart of Confucian ethics.[25] The focus of Confucian ethics is the perfectibility of human beings through self-effort. Biological growth is meaningless unless one tries to realize one's humanity through self-cultivation.[26] To become fully human is a recurring theme in Confucian thought. Because the endowment to be human is given at birth, everyone has the potential for growth. The way to perfectibility is not to acquire techniques from the external but rather to actualize the internal resources through self-cultivation.[27] Truth is to be found inside every individual. Grounded in Confucianism's cosmological understanding of the unity of heaven and earth, the task of learning transcends mere addition of knowledge. Rather, it transforms reality through thinking and hard work so that the mystery of the cosmos can be comprehended.

Confucian thought is the principal shaper of Chinese cultures. One may wonder how these ancient cultural values shape the Chinese mind when it comes to reading the Bible. I look for clues in the pietistic movement in Europe that shaped the missionaries' mission. One strand of Evangelicalism comes from the Holiness Movement of late nineteenth-century Europe.

23. Wei-Ming, *Humanity and Self-Cultivation*, 98.

24. Self-cultivation and social responsibility are not antithetical. In fact, it is difficult to separate the two because of their strong interdependence. Yet, for the sake of academic discussion, Confucian scholars emphasize self-cultivation as the necessary first step toward social involvement.

25. Wei-Ming, *Humanity and Self-Cultivation*, 71.

26. Wei-Ming, *Humanity and Self-Cultivation*, 35.

27. Wei-Ming, *Humanity and Self-Cultivation*, 26.

Influenced by pietism, missionaries to China preached a version of Christianity that stressed deeper Christian life through prayer and various pious practices. They stressed sanctified life and a higher spiritual state. To read the Bible through the lenses of personal conduct and spiritual growth sat well with the indigenous culture of their host country. Before the arrival of missionaries, Confucian ethics already taught inner constraint in personal development, high moral human conduct, and filial piety. It built on a positive assessment of human nature; through education, one can achieve *ren* (benevolence), *ji* (righteousness), and *li* (propriety). There is a certain compatibility between Western versions of Christianity and Confucian value.

The Chinese cultural respect for traditions also fits well with specific Christian doctrines. When it comes to the reading of the Bible, the doctrine of biblical inerrancy is still widely accepted by Chinese Christians. The doctrine stresses that the Bible is without errors, especially emphasizing the original manuscripts. This hermeneutical lens is seen as conforming to the traditions of the church. Confucian teachings, on the other hand, emphasize traditional values and ancestral practices. In *The Analects*, Confucius argued that not to change the way of one's parents is considered filial, that is, a good moral citizen. Respecting tradition and conforming to the status quo are considered virtues. The colonial hermeneutics brought by former missionaries was critiqued in Chinese seminaries in both Asia and Canada, and yet it continues to linger in the ways many grassroots Chinese Canadians approach the Bible.

Confucian culture tends to be patriarchal and Evangelical Christianity tends to support patriarchy. Such expressions of Christianity teach that men are the "head" of women. This teaching finds its cultural home in Confucianism as well. For example, in *Five Cardinals of Relationship*, Confucius portrays wives as subject to their husband as citizens are subject to the Emperor. The male is the head of the household. In the same way, based on a literal reading of the Bible, women have to exercise their gifts under the leadership of men. Chinese Evangelical churches still have a difficult time ordaining and calling women as pastors even though many call themselves open-minded Christians. Professional ordained ministry is still perceived to be best exercised by men. Wives are taught to be subject to the headship of their husbands. In this way, Confucian cultures and the imported European versions of Christianity share the same male-dominated ideas about leadership roles.

Commenting on the wider Asian Christian phenomenon in Anglo North America (USA and Canada), Chinese sociologist Fenggang Yang says Asian churches in North America serve as agents to preserve Asian cultures. By joining ethnic churches, Asian immigrants achieved *selective assimilation* where certain Asian cultural traits are preserved, especially the non-religious virtues such as filial piety.[28] *Selective assimilation* means taking control over the pace and aspects of assimilations.[29] It gives Asian North Americans power over how they like to conduct their lives. To illustrate, in terms of family obligations, Asian people already have a strong cultural foundation of honoring parents. They do not need Christianity to teach them. However, Christianity provides an explicit *religious* reason for observing filial piety—the love of God. In an individualistic society, where traditional family values are perceived to be collapsing, Chinese Evangelical churches provide a religious foundation that is reliable, certain, and authoritative for rejuvenating the Confucian ethics of filial piety. Morality, as informed by Confucianism, occupies a central role in how Chinese Christians approach the Bible. Through reading the Bible via the lens of personal spiritual growth, certain Confucian ideals are being fulfilled and carried on.

---

28. Not everything in Confucianism is desirable for preservation. For example, many Asian Christians accept the missionary teaching that ancestral worship is idolatry. They have no desire to preserve it. Asian people selectively pick and choose certain aspects of Confucianism that do not jeopardize the Christian faith.

29. Yang, *Chinese Christians*, 197.

Chinese in Canada: Immigration and Adaptation

Despite the fact that the experiences of Chinese Canadians are vastly diverse, there are also commonalities. We catch a glimpse of the issues Chinese face in Canada through the pens of Asian literature writers. Historically, Chinese Canadians have always struggled with issues of assimilation and the quest for identity. Sociologists point out that there is *structural* assimilation and *cultural* assimilation. Structural assimilation refers to the entrance of new immigrants into cliques, clubs, and institutions of the host society. Through participating in various institutions and infrastructure, immigrants achieve structural assimilation as members of the society. The ability to enter those institutions, however, depends upon the laws made by the dominant group. In the past, Chinese immigrants have experienced numerous denials of their rights as citizens in their new countries. In 1875, Chinese immigrants in Vancouver were denied voting rights. Other Asians in Anglo North America have experienced similar treatment.[30] In 1942, more than 120,000 Japanese men, women, and children were evacuated to the "internment camps." The US government confiscated their properties and deprived them of their constitutional rights. Cultural assimilation is even harder to achieve because it heightens the power differentials between new immigrants and long-time residents. It involves the assimilation of the values of the host society—which might imply giving up the cultural values of the newcomers. Immigrants and minorities are keenly aware of their vulnerability even if many of them are doing well financially. The ability to achieve cultural assimilation lies in the openness of the dominant cultural groups to welcome the entrance of newcomers and their cultural values. Many Chinese Canadians feel that they are marginalized because they carry different cultural norms.

Asian immigrants try hard to keep their cultures and languages. As visible minorities, their "racial uniformity" hinders them from being fully assimilated in the dominant society. No matter how good their English abilities are and how much they identify

30. Li, *Chinese in Canada*, 32.

themselves as Canadians, Chinese Canadians are easily recognized as *others*. At the same time, they often experience rejection in their communities of origin as being too westernized. Asian North Americans are caught *in-between* two worlds. As the late Professor Jung Young Lee says, "To be in-between two worlds means to be fully in neither. The marginal person who is placed between this two-world boundary feels like a non-being."[31]

There are additional internal factors. The "1.5 generation" poses intergenerational issues. Having grown up mostly in Canada, this generation has not shared in the traumatic experiences of their parents. They *share* the burdens of their parents but they have not personally *experienced* them. Such an intergenerational gap contributes to a sense of estrangement among the 1.5 generation—not only from the dominant Canadian culture but also from their Chinese families and heritage.[32] Because of the high rate of influx of Asian immigrants and their closer ties with Asia, it also further jeopardizes the relationship with those native-born Canadians who do not share the experiences of their parents to the same degree.[33]

In light of this social phenomenon, what is the role of Chinese Canadian churches? Can the church help Chinese to cope with racial tension? In what ways can the church assist in helping Chinese people be Canadians? Given the fact that issues of assimilation, racism, and the quest for identity occupy Chinese Canadians, they have also been struggling to define the role of the Chinese church in the USA and Canada.

There are psychological as well as social needs for Asian North Americans. In the case of Chinese immigrants, coming to Anglo North American means uprooting and re-establishing. This journey of resettlement is usually tense and uncertain, thus it produces "the intensification of the psychic basis of religious commitment."[34] Such needs push new immigrants to appreciate

31. Lee, *Marginality*, 45.
32. Lee, *Marginality*, 68.
33. Lee, *Marginality*, 67.
34. Yang, *Chinese Christians*, 30.

Chinese cultural values anew and, at the same time, look for the means to affirm those values in the new country. Another need is to find ways to enter the social, legal, and economic realm of their host country.

Even though Chinese churches are not considered the major agents of acculturation—at least not consciously—their adoption of the English language (for some) and Euro Canadian lifestyle helps their members to live harmoniously in Canada. As I indicated earlier, facing a multicultural, pluralistic, fast-paced, and uncertain society, many Chinese Christians find the conservative nature of Evangelicalism attractive. Evangelicalism offers ways to read the Bible that affirm the cultural desire for personal integrity and spiritual growth. Chinese Christians living in Canada are drawn to the Evangelical idea of absolute values and certainty. To clasp onto a faith tradition which teaches that Christians alone know the way of eternal truth offers its adherents a secure sense of acceptance and achievement. The Christian message of hope thus empowers many Chinese to deal with their pre-migration traumas and post-migration uncertainties in Canada.

The Christian message also meets their need to be accepted and valued. Chinese churches emphasize personal Bible study and small study groups. Bible study forms part of their spiritual practices as is strengthens their religious life and, in turn, enriches the relationship with one another. It is in these churches that they are able to see themselves as having accomplished something for which they experienced resistance in the secular world.[35] It is not surprising to see many Chinese churches approach the Bible predominantly through the lenses of morality. Sermons tend to focus on personal faith issues and individual integrity. Although the Bible contains strong teachings on social justice, Chinese Canadians are neither drawn to those writings nor considered politically active.

Sigurd Kaiser, a New Testament professor in China, observed that sermons in China carry a strong dualism of heaven and earth

35. Yang, *Chinese Christians*, 94.

and are heavily evangelistic.[36] People who have theological train-ing in the West (Western Europe and Anglo North America) will find text proofing is common with very little historical exegesis. Sermons often do not address social issues but rather meet the existential needs of the people. One may suggest that such ten-dencies take place because the audience in China has low levels of education; sometimes even the preachers may not have received adequate institutional training. While some sectors of the popu-lation display low levels of education, for many, such tendencies are understandable when we consider the impact of the built-in Confucian cultural ideals; these fit very well with the ontological pragmatic concerns of Chinese culture.

Chinese churches—at least from the perspective of Chinese parents—preserve Chinese cultural values while participating in religious activities that shaped the civilization of Western world. That is, Chinese Canadian churches both preserve and maintain ethnic differences. Not all Chinese Christians think the same way. Liberal-minded Asian Christians who care about social justice exist, though they are a very small minority. Christian educator Russell Moy argues that the task of religious educators is to be aware of the social and racial ideology of the dominant society and to expand the teachings of the Bible.[37] Moy extends the challenge to the wider North American society, confronting racism in their teaching of the Bible. He argues that the Bible is often taught from a Euro-USA standpoint and neglects the voices of the people of color. To com-bat racism, this challenge is extended to the dominant groups that hold power and privilege. Many Chinese Canadians join churches because of a mixture of complex sociological factors and religious reasons. Concerning theology, many Chinese Christians under-stand Christian churches as embodying the only *true religion* God intends, as was taught by the previous generation of missionaries, pastors, and theologians. Sociologically, ethnic churches function as safe havens, affirm Chinese cultural values, and provide the pro-phetic voices of marginalized Chinese people.

36. Kaiser, "Church Growth in China," 39.

37. Moy, "American Racism," 121–25.

Second, third, and fourth generations of Chinese Canadian Christians are showing signs of change. As much as the first-generation Chinese Christian immigrants want their children to practice faith the same way as they do, these local born Chinese Christians, having grown up in Canada, have daily exposure to different ways of thinking and being. They grew up with many classmates who exercise different religions and beliefs. It is not easy to expect strict conformation to their parents' wishes.

Nam Soon Song—a professor of Christian education at Knox College, University of Toronto—and her colleagues conducted a research study called "Religious Attitudes and Commitment Among 1.5 and Second Generation Asian-Canadian Protestant Young Adults."[38] The study took two years to complete. The team surveyed 300 Asian university students, studying mostly in Ontario, with 74 questions. Out of these 300 students, from age 17 to 29, 115 called themselves Chinese, 150 Korean, and 35 Taiwanese. The responders were invited to comment on their church experiences while they were in high school as well as their current church and spiritual life. They were also invited to comment on their expectation of church and youth ministry. This is a significant qualitative research study that gives us a glimpse of those who grew up in Canada. Initial findings suggest that the Bible continues to serve an important role for these Chinese Canadians, although only ten percent of respondents say they are reading the Bible as an ongoing spiritual practice. Most of the respondents say they attend Bible studies less than once a month, yet many of them do attend once a month. The data seems to suggest that, at least conceptually, Chinese Canadians affirm the importance of reading the Bible. This may be due to years of attending church with their parents, although only a small percentage of them now practice as an ongoing discipline. When asked, "In what ways has church life helped you?" the majority ranked moral values at the top of their list.

38. Nam Soon Sung and her colleagues conducted a qualitative research concerning second generation and 1.5 generation Canadian Chinese. At the time of this writing, however, the report has not been published yet.

A significant number of respondents yearn for the church to be a safe place to discuss the hot issues of the day. Some hope that the church will become more open, less judgmental, and welcome liberal theology. Not surprisingly, the second generation of Canadian Christians desire more diversity, openness, inclusiveness, and safety. If Chinese Christian churches take these findings seriously, they will need to examine the ways in which they can create safe spaces for dialogue, where critical and thoughtful exchange can take place. Rather than imposing doctrinal positions, moral values, and ready-made answers, Chinese Canadian churches can potentially offer a safe, dialogical space, where the sincere, nonjudgmental exploration of viewpoints and ideas is experienced. Can this be achieved? Chinese Canadian Christians need to do some soul-searching to see whether the assumed Confucian cultural values and deeply held theological positions can be opened up for review and negotiation.

Concluding Thoughts

Chinese Canadian Christians deeply love the Bible. Many of them study it at home and in small groups. The way they understand and read it is, in large measure, still influenced by the past teachings of Western missionaries. In order to persuade Chinese to accept Christianity, Western missionaries condemned Chinese religions and some of their cultural practices. In addition, those same missionaries taught that all the world religions—except for Christianity—were wrongheaded and not worth practicing. After two hundred years of evangelization, many Chinese Christians have internalized this imperialistic message. This mentality is what shapes the way many Chinese Christians read the Bible.

In the same way, this tradition of honoring the Bible also finds its way in the deeply treasured Confucian culture. Teaching as a profession is culturally respected. Although the missionary enterprise of the colonial era has been criticized at the academic level, at the grassroots level, Chinese Canadians express gratitude for Western missionaries' love and bravery toward Chinese people.

Coupled with the strong Confucian emphasis on morality and self-improvement, Chinese Canadians continue to find the Bible to be a great source of inspiration for individual growth. They tend to read the Bible through the lens of morality. These lenses become important when they resettle in Canada, especially for first-generation immigrants. To find comfort and certainty in a new land, they turn to the Bible and the church for resources to rejuvenate their Confucian ideals.

Many Chinese Canadians have deep Asian cultural and religious roots, whether Confucianism, Taoism, Buddhism, or other folk religions. These roots remain the case even when many of them were born in Canada. Such deep cultural roots and practices are passed on by their parents at home and by growing up attending religious places of worship. Although many Chinese Canadians attend Christian churches, Chinese Canadians continue to be guided by their own cultural values. The way to be Christian is not *either-or* but *both-and* in terms of cultural practices and even deeply held religious beliefs. Confucian ideals and biblical visions are entertained simultaneously. They search for common ground to accommodate each other. To observe both Confucian values and to be a Christian is not seen as contradictory or incompatible. The Bible's moral teachings on love, service, and faithfulness support the very teachings of Confucianism. Chinese Canadians read the Bible to find their affinity toward morality supported.

The Bible, however, is essentially Jewish literature, composed in a Jewish cultural background and social environment through complex processes of collecting and editing. Language and culture are closely linked and cannot be separated. The prophetic biblical traditions entail more than our morality and individual status before God, they also carry strong voices of social justice. To honor the Bible, one cannot uplift the pietistic-moral lens without equally uplifting its social justice dimension. Whether the Bible is viewed as trustworthy or not, readers will need to have a deeper understanding of it, regarding the sociocultural situations and assumptions under which it was formed. The meaning of a text often reflects its readers. With this in mind, when Chinese Canadian Christians read the Bible, it is essentially a cross-cultural experience. While it is unrealistic to remove the indigenous cultural lenses of its readers, it is crucial to identify the readers' working assumptions.

3

Toward a Version of "Narratival Hermeneutics"—Reading Ecclesiastes Ethno-Culturally with a Chinese Lens

Selfhood, Diaspora Experience, and the Search for Meaning

Barbara M. Leung Lai

From the Changing Landscape to My Present Undertaking

THREE FACTORS SHAPE THE incentive of my present endeavor: Toward *"a"* Chinese Canadian version of narratival hermeneutics as it relates to the reading of a strange book—Ecclesiastes.

First, teaching "Wisdom Literature" as one of my signature courses over the past two decades has continuously shaped my approach to reading—from purely cognitive to that of experiential and perspectival. As a Chinese Canadian woman, reading strategies employed in my interpretation of Ecclesiastes have been referred to as examples of culture-specific or ideological-critical readings.[1] This

---

1. See my two recent publications on Ecclesiastes: Leung Lai, "Voice and Ideology," 265–78; and Leung Lai, "Preacher," 214–16.

is affirming and yet, at the same time, puzzling. In the course of this undertaking, I have asked myself several times the extent that my Chinese culture, gender, and Canadian situatedness may shape the way that I engage in the reading of this book.

Second, methodologically located in the *"interdisciplinary"* terrain of the social sciences and biblical studies, I have beheld wonders and experienced enlightening moments while journeying along this multi-disciplinary path, witnessing the *never* exhausting *but* ever-expanding, ever-enriching meaning-significance of the biblical text to the community of readers.

Third, adopting John Goldingay's *"narrative" approach* to constructing theology based on the Hebrew Bible,[2] we are encouraged to engage ourselves in theological inquiries arising out of humanity's collective lived experience under the sun with an elevated dosage of vigor and vitality. Engaging in this endeavor, I have come to a fuller understanding of the interface between perceiving "dogma" as the most exciting "drama" in the Christian Church *and* "narrative" as a dynamic and powerful approach to constructing biblical theologies, especially for the Hebrew Bible. While highlighting the rich *cultural mix* of Canada and diverse Canadian interpretive traditions are the primary objectives of this collaborative project, as a Hebrew Bible scholar, I will add another dimension in reading Ecclesiastes—laying "raw" in front of readers the kind of "helplessness" and "perplexity" in humanity's search for meaning from the perspective of a Chinese reader.

In the following discussion, I seek to address two questions:

1. Under the rubrics of text, culture, and contextual biblical interpretation: *In what ways would "a" Chinese Canadian reading shed light on the meaning-significance of Ecclesiastes to the community of (Chinese) readers?*

2. Rooted in humanity's collective lived experience under the sun (i.e., "text and experience" as Smith-Christopher has coined the term)[3] and in the broader context of text and

2. See Goldingay, *Old Testament Theology*.
3. See Smith-Christopher, *Text and Experience*.

praxis: *In what ways would the outcome of a culture-specific reading contribute towards "a" paradigm of "How to Live" from the book of Ecclesiastes?*

Text, Culture, and Contextual Biblical Interpretation

"In what ways would 'a' Chinese Canadian reading shed light on the meaning-significance of the Book of Ecclesiastes to the community of (Chinese) readers?"

The book of Ecclesiastes is, in essence, a self-narrated "I-Text." Reading and hearing the "I" voice of Qohelet pronouncing boldly the summary appraisal, "Utterly senseless! Everything is meaningless!" captivates the mind and arouses the emotive response of the reader. This essay focuses on the interface of "text and culture" and "text and lived experience." I seek to explore the ways that (1) the Chinese concept of self/selfhood; (2) the idea of "emptiness/meaninglessness" in the Chinese mind; (3) the virtue of "perseverance," upheld as one of the most esteemed qualities of a person in Chinese philosophy; and (4) the diaspora experience of Chinese immigrants in Canada may impact how Chinese readers read and understand the meaning-significance of the book. It is hoped that this endeavor may provide "*a*" demonstrated example of the vibrant dynamics and power in the "art" and "science" of "narratival hermeneutics"—a reading that takes seriously the flesh and blood collective lived-experience of the community of Chinese readers.

Four ports of entry can be identified toward a Chinese Canadian ethno-cultural reading of Ecclesiastes: (1) The Chinese concept of "self" in dialogue with Qohelet's "I"-voice; (2) The Chinese idea of "emptiness/meaninglessness" in response to the bold pronouncement in the summary appraisal: "Utterly meaningless!"; (3) The notion of "perseverance" in the Chinese philosophy of life and the adaptation of a "cross-graining" reading strategy; and (4) The collective lived-experience (the "Mega-Text") of the first generation Chinese immigrant community interacting with Qohelet's exploration in life.

The Chinese Concept of Self in Dialogue
with Qohelet's "I"-Voice

Interdisciplinary studies on the "self" represent a variety of goal-oriented approaches.[4] They are methodologically eclectic, and generally postmodern.[5] The end products of this "multiple-diverse-postmodern" inquiring situation may cast new light on to the interconnectedness of self, community, the shaping of one's life-context,[6] and the narratival interpretive thrust in reading Ecclesiastes.

First, self-construction and identity are found in the community and in the communal experience. It is not in the transcendence of society to search for a single, private self.[7] Self of an individual character is formed by the surrounding community, and this could be referred to as one's communal lived-experience, shaping one's life context. *Second*, as to the relationship between self and narrative, it is the "ability of narrative to verbalize and situate experience as text."[8] *Third*, the psychological approach to the self-concept presents strong empirical evidence in support of the existence of the "other" in its construction.

This pluralistic model of the self perceives an individual as inextricably in dialogue with others.[9] It is interesting to note that approaches to the concept of self in psychology and the humanities converge at this point. Also, this *plural* self-idea bears notable

4. For a general orientation of the multi-disciplinary scholarly research on the concept of self, see Leung Lai, *Through the "I"-Window*, 30–36.

5. See Callero, "Society of the Self," 15–33, esp. 116.

6. Or in the words of Anthony C. Thiselton, "Life-worlds" (see Thiselton, *New Horizons*, 247–52). David R. Blumenthal draws on the same concept and refers to the whole flesh and blood lived-experience of an individual as a "text-of-life." See Blumenthal, *Facing an Abusing God*, 6. See also my own development of the concept in Leung Lai, "Psalm 44," 418–31.

7. Bjork, *Novels of Toni Morrison*, vii.

8. Deborah Schiffrin's approach to narrative analysis brings about the power and effectiveness of constructing the self and identity for individuals. As she concludes, it is the "ability of narrative to verbalize and situate experience as text" (Schiffrin, "Narrative as Self-Portrait," 167).

9. See Brown and Cooper, *Plural Self*.

resemblance to the Russian literary scholar Mikhael Bakhtin's theory of the "dialogic self."[10] The context of this dialogue is within the "Grand Narrative"—the collective lived-experience of humanity under the sun.

Remarkably, the Chinese concept of the "self" shares much in common with the results of the above investigation. In traditional Chinese culture, the *autonomy* of the "self" is not recognized. Taken negatively, people often say that a Chinese person has "no self" and that the notion of "private self" is not encouraged. The Chinese "self" can be described as both interdependent and sociocentric (or situation-centered).[11] Adopting this Chinese concept of the "self," the juxtaposition of self, community, and life-context forms the theoretical backbone of my ethno-cultural reading of Ecclesiastes as a first generation Chinese Canadian. On the one hand, moving from the Chinese idea of the non-existence of the "autonomous self" to the postmodern ethos of "free self" has been a long and difficult path.[12] One has to consciously put the previously subdued Chinese "private self" to the foreground of interaction. Yet, on the other hand, this culture-specific mentality paves the way for Chinese immigrants to adapt ourselves to the postmodern concept of self, one that is pluralistic and in constant dialogue with our environment—the "others." In other words, my reading cannot be isolated from my community's reading perspectives as my own experience is a slice of the reality contributing to the community's flesh and blood collective lived-experience.

Qohelet's "I" is constantly in active interaction with his surroundings through the dynamics of the cycle of *"seeing-reflecting*

---

10. See Bakhtin, *Dialogic Imagination.*

11. See Hsu, "Self in Cross-Cultural Perspective," 24–55.

12. Postmodern theorists differ considerably about the determinacy of the context and agency of the self. As a commonly accepted maxim, however, the postmodern self is socially constructed, fluidic, and multiple. Randy G. Litchfield describes the way that the self "is not centered in one location, but decentered across many social settings . . . We are many selves that must be orchestrated into coherence, an ongoing process that we recognize as our identity" (Litchfield, "Rethinking Local Bible Study," 236). For an opposite view, see the same text, 236–37.

-perceiving-concluding" (see Eccl 1:14–18; 2:1–26; 3:16–22; 4:1–12, 15–16; 5:13–20; 6:1–12; 7:15–18, 25–29; 8:10–12, 14–17; 9:1–18; 10:5–15). Rooted in the Chinese mentality, the idea of corporate personality shapes the path for Chinese readers to initiatively orchestrate our individual "text-of-life"—the "small self" (*Xiao Wo*) into the bigger whole—the "Mega-Text/Grand Narrative" (*Da Wo*). This interconnectedness of the components of "self-community-'life-context'-narrative" becomes the *interpretive thrust* of my ethnocultural reading. At the same time, I seek to exemplify the vibrant dynamics of "*a*" version of narratival hermeneutics.

The Chinese Concept of "Emptiness/Meaninglessness"
in Response to the Bold Announcement in the Summary Appraisal:
"Everything is utterly meaningless!"

There is no equivalent term for "meaningless/senselessness" in Chinese Philosophy. Buddhism does emphasize "emptiness," which may resemble the meaning of the Hebrew word הבל (*hebel*, "vanity") used many times in Ecclesiastes. The Chinese perception of "meaninglessness" is not so much a philosophical concept; it is rather engrained in one's lived-experience. On the larger scale, the "cultural revolution" (1966–1976) and the June 4 Massacre in Tiananmen Square (1989) were the darkest, most unforgettable moments in Chinese modern history. The drastic political changes, famine, national disasters, civil wars, and, most recently, the extent of the helplessness felt by the people of Hong Kong over the failure of the umbrella democratic movement,[13] have all left a lasting impact on the global Chinese diaspora communities. With sheer disappointment towards the government of Hong Kong/China and a deep sense of powerlessness, immigrant families and the 1.5 generation (youths) in Canada know very well the meaning of "meaninglessness!"

13. Perceived as the first democratic movement of Hong Kong (China's "Special Legislative Region"), which was supported by and involved the majority of its citizens—people from all walks of life and professions.

The "I"-voice of Qohelet invites all readers to identify with him the kind of vanity and senselessness that he has witnessed under the sun, and the emotive impact that these "commonalities" bear on him—"everything is utterly meaningless" (Eccl 1:1, 12–14; 2:1)! The magnitude of the absurdity in life (Eccl 2:7; 3:16–17; 7:15; 8:12–14) drives Qohelet to a weighty summary appraisal—seeking to make some sense out of the nonsensicality in life is like "chasing after the wind"—doomed to fail! What he shares with readers are not merely deep, self-reflective statements; the weight of his out-cries is found in the burdensome commonalities that he embraces (in all "flesh") and his address to slices of the reality of the "Grand Narrative" in which all readers (Chinese or non-Chinese) share and contribute to crafting—again, with our flesh and blood.[14]

As I put my "I" (small self [Xiao Wo]), into the commu-nal "we" (big self [Da Wo]) of Chinese readers, I have found the eruption and intensity of Qohelet's *"outcry"* both enlightening and liberating. In a culture that values the communal dimen-sion of lived-experience and discourages the autonomy of the "self"—reading Ecclesiastes and hearing the "I"-voice of Qohelet provide the body of *"language"* for Chinese readers to cry out boldly as we resonate with the rational mind-set and the emotive disturbance of Qohelet. Like the psalmist of Psalm 44, Chinese faith communities are encouraged to reclaim the costly loss of lament—"crying out heavenwards towards God" out of our col-lective and respective situatedness.

Text and Lived-Experience and the Chinese Notion of Perseverance

In rethinking contextual issues, it is a commonly accepted maxim that "all content is subject to context" and "there is no text without context."[15] Meaning-significance is context-bound, but context is boundless. Appropriating the collective message of Ecclesiastes

14. Perspectives here are drawn from Leung Lai, "Preacher," 214–16.

15. Fetzer and Oishi, *Context and Contexts*, 171.

to the context of the Chinese diaspora community is, in essence, a "context-selection" enterprise. In a culture that regards "eating bitterness" (literally) or "perseverance" (conceptually) as one of its highest virtues, Chinese readers have been nurtured with a better capacity for enduring suffering (to the extent of extreme trials in life) and coping with difficulties in one's life-context. In the case of Ecclesiastes, Chinese readers can have a better grip of the core message engrained in the book—*"embracing co-existing dialectic tensions is the way to live!"* To translate this to the meaning-significance for Chinese readers, it could be dynamically articulated as follows: instead of finding a way to cope, the Chinese diaspora community would tend to have acquired the inner strength to sustain ourselves as we embrace dialectic tensions in our individual and communal life-contexts. Deeply rooted in Chinese ideology, the ability of "sustaining in tension" is more esteemed than that of "resolving tension." This culturally- and ideologically-shaped approach to life and its sheer reality (i.e., life is complex and full of dialectic tensions) is acquired through the passing on of family legacy and cultural values.

Text and Praxis: Toward "a" Paradigm of "How to Live"

In what ways would the outcome of a Chinese Canadian culture-specific reading contribute towards "a" paradigm of "How to Live"?

The discussion in the previous sections provides a community-based and ideologically/culturally-shaped profile of the Chinese reader. As a point of departure, I will focus on the juxtaposition of the Chinese community's capacity in embracing co-existing tensions in life and a newly emerged reading strategy for the book of Ecclesiastes (i.e., reading "cross the grains"[16]). On the one hand, this is a unique perspectival reading of the book. On the other hand, this reading may potentially add yet another layer of depth

---

16 See Leung Lai, "Voice and Ideology," 265–78; and Leung Lai, "Preacher," 214–16.

to the meaning-significance of Ecclesiastes as appropriated by the Chinese community. Not only it is meant to provide an exemplar of "narratival hermeneutics," but also, I aim at demonstrating "*a*" Chinese-specific version on *"How to Live"*—one that is rooted in the collective lived-experience of the Chinese diaspora community and is being brought to the foreground through the vehicle of a "cross-graining" reading strategy.

Reading Ecclesiastes Ideological-Critically with a Chinese Lens: Reading "Cross the Grains"

Voice and Ideology

The interface of voice and ideology is firmly established in the field of biblical studies.[17] Ecclesiastes is predominantly an "I"-text,[18] but it is also a polyphony (multi-voiced). Identification of the different voices represented in Ecclesiastes has been an area of interest especially in the recent past.[19] Incorporating earlier attempts, Kyle R. Greenwood has provided a precise analysis of the three voices in the book.[20]

The *first* voice is the collective voice of the sages, referred to as the "true voice of wisdom," which primarily speaks in the second-person imperative. It represents the wisdom tradition in Ancient Israel (or embedded ideology in the text). The *second* voice is the voice of Qohelet, speaking as Solomon, in the captivating first-person "I"-voice. It represents the reshaped ideology of Qohelet, which is cast in sharp contrast with the embedded ideology of the text (the wisdom tradition). The *third* voice serves as the "Frame

17. See Leung Lai, *Through the "I"-Window*, 37–39; Greenwood, "Debating Wisdom," 476–91; Landy, "Vision and Voice," 19–36; and Landy, "Impersonal Voice," 113–51.

18. Places where the character speaks in the first person "I"-voice.

19. See Holmstedt, "אני ולבי," 1–27; and Bartholomew, *Ecclesiastes*, 75–83. In the latter volume, Bartholomew summarized and responded to Michael Fox's analysis of the speaking voices in Ecclesiastes. See Fox, "Frame-Narrative," 83–106

20. Greenwood, "Debating Wisdom, 476–91.

Narrator," and it is found in the third person sections of chapters 1 and 12.[21] My reading leads me to *add* another two to these identifiable voices: (1) the voice of the epilogist (Eccl 12:9–14) who seeks to provide a quick fix to the tensions surfacing from chapter 1 to 12:8 through Qohelet's search for meaning; and (2) the inner voice of Qohelet, which emerges from the imaginary dialogue within the monologues—e.g., "I said with my heart saying, I, behold"[22] (Eccl 1:16; 2:1, 15; 3:17).

Along the above stated interpretive path, there is yet another voice: the interpretive voice of the Chinese reader, representing the *readerly ideology* they bring to the text and interacting with the embedded textual ideologies of traditional wisdom and that of Qohelet. The textual dynamics are such that there are at least *two levels of readerly response*. Through Qohelet's compelling "I"-voice, readers are invited to respond ideologically-critically to his summary appraisals as he interacts with the traditional wisdom. Moreover, the reader also responds to the epilogist's attempt at "making-it-right" (Eccl 12:9–14), defending the traditional wisdom ideology. This *readerly ideology* is, in essence, an interpretive choice.

Considering polyphony as the characteristic feature of Ecclesiastes, the analysis and textual dynamics of narration, reflection, inner debate, explanation, and resolution (especially regarding the role of the epilogist in the book) take on new dimensions of meaning. The intertwining of speaking voices in Ecclesiastes provides a framing for reading and hearing the text,[23] making this ideological-critical path a vibrant, self-engaging endeavor for the Chinese reader.

21. I see the voice of the epilogist in chapter 12 as another distinct voice, seeking to provide a quick fix towards resolution of the existing tensions that surfaced in chapters 1–11.

22. It is a triple emphatic use of the preacher's "I"-voice here. As Adele Berlin has noted, הנה ("Behold") functions almost like an "interior monologue," an "internalized viewpoint" that provides a kind of "interior vision." See Berlin, *Poetics and Interpretation*, 62–63.

23. For texts of a polyphonic nature, the practice of "hearing the text" (i.e. "the hermeneutics of hearing") is perhaps a necessity. See Snodgrass, "Reading to Hear," 1–32.

As a highly reflective people, the Chinese reader has adopted a worldview that life is made up of a plurality of competing choices (just like the multiplicity of contending speaking voices represented in the book). The Chinese philosophy of life and its ideals are grounded in centuries of rich wisdom tradition (or a "Mega-Text" crafted with layers of depth through the collective lived-experience of the ancient Chinese community). We all carry the baggage of traditional Chinese values (e.g., the "cause and effect" approach to life: "be good and you will be rewarded with goodness" in the so-called "order of things"). Against the traditional Israelite wisdom of the "Two-Way Doctrine/Blessing and Cursing" (see Deut 11:26–28; 28; Prov 3:33), Qohelet wrestles with the nonsensical in life in his self-engaged explorations (Eccl 6:1–6; 7:15; 8:14–17). In like manner, Chinese readers resist coming to terms with the epilogist's overly-simplistic attempt to provide a quick-fix to "making-it-right" by defending the traditional wisdom (Eccl 12:9–14). We are being compelled to echo with the summary appraisal uttered by Qohelet: "Everything is meaningless" if we lay "raw" our collective lived-experience under the sun against the ideals in traditional Chinese wisdom. The vibrant interpretive thrust for a Chinese reader could be found in the liberating "space"—crying out boldly in affirming the absurdity in life and its nonsensicality. Crossing borders between the home and the host culture, Chinese immigrant families have to go through the journey of alienation, adaptation, assimilation, and, for some, re-orientation in life, just like the competing speaking voices/ideologies—pleasure or pain, success or failure, blessing or cursing—are among the possibilities of this border-crossing experience in the diaspora.

Reading "Cross the Grains"

Using the imagery of woodworking, just like wood, all texts have grains or directionality. Here, I have picked up Carol A. Newsom's "plywood" analysis, but with a more focused appropriation.[24]

---

24. See Newsom, "Reflections on Ideological Criticism," 553–57.

There are two conventional reading strategies that could be applied to the reading of any given text: reading "with the grain" and reading "against the grain." Engaging Ecclesiastes calls for a reading that is "cross the grains." "Cross-graining" is applied to the production of plywood, piecing together layers (veneers) of adjacent piles and gluing the wood grain at right angles to each other. As such, a high-quality, high-strength wood panel is formed. More specifically, plywood is bonded with grains running against one another, perpendicular to the grain direction. Bonded together, several thin layers of wood are stronger than one single, thick layer of wood. This produces the strongest kind of wood that is hard to bend. As a Chinese reader, I have found this "cross-graining" imagery quite fitting for a reading strategy that incorporates not only both conventional "against the grain" and "with the grain" but also has the potential of moving into the multilayered, more enriched meanings of the book.

The narratival-hermeneutical thrust could be found in two levels of Qohelet's reflection in life. *First*, Qohelet is interacting "against the grain" of the ideologies embedded in traditional Israelite Wisdom (his "pretext"). *Second*, Qohelet is inviting all readers (his first audience and contemporary Chinese readers) from our different ideological locations to respond to his discourse "with the grain" through his compelling "I"-voice.[25] This involves consideration of the roles of both the narrator (Eccl 1:1–11; 7:27)[26] and the epilogist (Eccl 12:9–14).[27]

Reading as an engaged reader seeking to appropriate the book's message to the life-context of the Chinese community, four ideologies could be identified in this "cross-graining" endeavor: (1) the ideology of traditional Chinese wisdom to which we are interacting "against the grain"—i.e., "be good and you will be blessed" and this is "the order of things"; (2) the multilayered ideology

25. This could be considered as a unique example in the Hebrew Bible.

26. For a detailed analysis of the narrative structure of Ecclesiastes, esp. the "frame narrator" in 1:2, 7:27; and 12:8–14, see Christianson, *Time to Tell*, 45–50.

27. See esp. Shead, "Reading Ecclesiastes," 86–91.

upheld by Qohelet and embedded in our community's collective lived experience—e.g., life is utterly meaningless in spite of all human efforts and enjoy life while we can (see the *carpe diem* short sayings: Eccl 9:7–9; 11:7–9); (3) be sustained in dialectic tensions in life while entertaining the reshaped ideology proposed by the narrator—i.e., defending the traditional wisdom and its values— and especially by the epilogist's quick-fix approach to "making-it-right" (Eccl 12:8–14); and (4) the *readerly ideology* that results from "cross-graining"—navigating through the options of one's interpretive choice and negotiating by placing the existing interpretive tensions side-by-side as an *"enriched" whole*.

While Qohelet's ideology clashes with the ideology ingrained in traditional wisdom, Chinese readers are left with *three interpretive choices*: (1) being drawn to the affirmation of the preacher's ideology—the absurdity of life overarching the "order of things"[28]; (2) adopting the perspectives proposed by the narrator and epilogist, reaffirming the reality of the two-way doctrine, or one that is "cause-effect" oriented (Eccl 12:13–14; cf. Deut 11:26–28); or (3) bringing another *readerly ideology* into the reading through embracing, rejecting (especially in refusing to accept the epilogist's over-simplistic way of providing a quick-fix to defend traditional wisdom[29]), or reshaping Qohelet's and the epilogist's ideology through cross-graining. Like the production of plywood, with wood grains running against each other ("cross-graining"), putting the two conflicting ideologies together (that is, [1] and [2] above) has the potential of coming up with a more enriched, multi-layered meaning-significance of the collective message of the book. As a Chinese reader in the diaspora, I have made my

28. The same dynamics and alternatives have been spelled out in Walton, "Reading Qohelet," 130.

29. Michael Fox supports the idea that in an effort to protect Qohelet, the epilogist is combining הבל and ירא to present a composite view of reality: fear of God is the right attitude, along with the trust that God is "just" (see Fox, "Frame Narrative," 83–106). However, to Roland Murphy, reading Ecclesiastes from the perspective of the epilogist as exemplified above is an "oversimplification" of the preacher's ideological conflicts as echoed everywhere in his "I"-voice. See Murphy, *Ecclesiastes*, lxv.

interpretive choice: life is complex, and the plurality of existing dialectic tensions is simply part of life's reality. They are "givens." Embracing tension gives diction to *"How to Live."*

What Would a Reading That Is "Cross the Grains" Yield?

For an average engaged reader, reading the whole book of Ecclesiastes "with the grain" or "against the grain" are both possible and natural. The reflective "I" voice of Qohelet has the power to entice readers' engagement into his "I"-discourse, reading his treatise "with the grain." As a Chinese reader, however, I find the role of the epilogist is at odds with the deep, reflective momentum in this "I"-discourse. In a way, it disrupts the vein of Qohelet's argument—that there is no order of things in human experience, just total chaos. In this respect, reading the book of Ecclesiastes "against the grain," the epilogist makes an overly simplistic attempt toward a quick-fix for the limits of wisdom. As with the book of Job, it is an open ending. Readers find it difficult to come to a closure of the senselessness of life laid raw in front of us with such a heavy statement—"Let us hear the conclusion of the whole matter: Fear God and keep his commandments—for this applies to every person" (12:13). This conclusion *deconstructs* the whole ethos spelled out in Qohelet's burdensome "I." It *silences* the inquiring voice of all "faith-seeking-understanding" inquiries! One thing stands out clearly—for the book of Ecclesiastes, either reading "against the grain" or "with the grain" are both inadequate for grasping the totality of the book's message.

As a Chinese reader, I seek to further spell out the vibrant dynamics of my *interpretive path*: reading "cross the grains." Two distinct ideologies surface in the two different directional readings exemplified above. *First,* Qohelet holds on to the ideology that all attempts to search for the order of things in this chaotic world will be met with sheer disappointment. *Second,* the ideology ingrained in the text—"fear God and keep his commandments"—is required for all humanity. Qohelet seeks to embrace both, in all "flesh," but finds it burdensome and oppressive. The epilogist seeks to defend the latter by underscoring twice in the "afterword" of Qohelet's "I"-discourse: "And more than that . . ." (Eccl 12:9) and "more than these . . ." (Eccl 12:12). Two sets of ideologies are presented side by side. My attempt is neither to harmonize or synthesize the two conflicting ideologies nor to pick one against the other as a hermeneutical choice. A reading that "crosses the grains" of both ideologies may help to put the two conflicting ideologies together, side by side, as *co-existing realities.* Moreover, the nature of these co-existing tensions is of a polar nature. The woodworking imagery of the production of plywood fits in beautifully with this endeavor. By placing the veneers with wood grains running against each other and gluing them together at right angles perpendicular to each other, I aim at uncovering the existence of the *many, cross-graining fibers* that constitute Ecclesiastes—that is, the collective message of the book. Shaped by our cultural and ideological values, Chinese readers could have the capacity to engage in this "cross-graining" reading endeavor.

Toward "a" Paradigm of "How to Live"

The purpose of this "cross-graining" reading trajectory or directionality is not gearing towards resolutions, but the *"how"* of embracing life. As stated previously, the Chinese reader is nurtured with the kind of capacity to embrace life along with all its complexities. In this sense, reading Ecclesiastes within the contextual situatedness of Chinese readers in the diaspora, it appears to be a profoundly significant book—providing *"a"* version towards a practical theology on *how* to live our lives. With the shared *common denominator* of the "collective lived-experience under the sun," we echo each of the outpoured cries of Qohelet and the deep-rooted, burdensome (though occasionally uplifting) concluding statements he utters. The shared ideological reflections of Qohelet are not constructed sophistically or after a rigid frame of reference. Rather, it is rooted in the "flesh-and-blood" collective lived-experience of all humanity. This reflects the true essence of narratival hermeneutics. Embracing co-existing tensions (at times of polar nature) is the *way* to conduct our lives. Amidst the harshness of life, there are still glimpses of uplifting momentum (e.g., Eccl 7:29; 8:12b; 11:7–9; 12:9–12).

Afterword: Mapping the Term of "Narratival Hermeneutics"

This discourse is my small contribution to the mapping of narratival hermeneutics—laying-out a robust drama of the dogma rooted in humanity's collective lived-experience. I have asked, what are the "normative" claims that could be drawn from a gendered, culture-specific, narratival reading of the book of Ecclesiastes in Canada? In hammering out a reading strategy for Ecclesiastes, what looms large in this endeavor is that it not only addresses the mind cognitively, but also, appeals to the heart. As a Chinese woman and biblical scholar, I have learned something essential regarding the task of biblical interpretation: it is inherently a vibrant and vigorous engagement of the whole "self"—mind, will, emotion, and imagination. As I put my Chinese "small self" (*Xiao Wo*) into the "bigger self" (*Da Wo*), or alternatively, as I engage my flesh and blood experience in my community's collective lived-experience, I can identify several layers of connectedness ("cross the grains") in this Grand Narrative of human life.

4

Inter-Positioning

A Korean-Canadian Homiletical Theologian's
Reading the Story of Jephthah's Daughter

HYERAN KIM-CRAGG

Preface: The Narrative of the Position of Sitting

My most comfortable position for work is sitting down
with both legs crossed. I take this position in my chair al-
most all the time, for listening to students in class, writing
and marking papers in front of the computer, engaging
in faculty meetings, singing at choir practice, watching a
movie in a theatre, and so on. This sitting position needs
to be negotiated and adjusted, depending upon the kind of
chair I am in and how much room I have in relation to the
space of others. My sitting position is never fixed but al-
ways changes and shifts.[1] I come from Korea where sitting
on the floor with that position is common. People there
cook, eat, talk, and even worship in that position. I have
observed and learned this position and have developed it
as my own. I have also been influenced by other religions,

---

1. I have articulated this position of sitting still in "Palm Sunday," 96.

including Buddhism, which requires such a position as a spiritual practice. You may say this is my culture. Indeed, I feel blessed by this pluralistic heritage. But the blessing comes with its own challenges.

One challenge that I experience relates to the adoption of our Euro Canadian culture. Migrating to Canada, seeking to further my education, I had to negotiate my position to fit into the chair culture. The Euro Canadian chair culture, though convenient in many ways, caused me discomfort. Part of that discomfort was due to the fact that most chairs are designed to fit relatively tall people. Chairs (non-adjustable ones) normalize tall people. Many people—including children—who are less than 5 feet tall can identify with the discomfort of having their feet dangling above the floor while sitting on the chair. The inflexible and unaccommodating chair also forces us to dismiss the differences in the size and shape of bodies and cultural formations, while pushing everyone to sit in a fixed way.

Introduction

THIS ESSAY, USING THE experience of the sitting-position narrated above as a metaphor, proposes an "inter-positioning" approach to interpreting the Bible. By inter-positioning, I mean the intentional crossing of disciplines in which I engage in this paper; from a homiletical theologian to engaging hermeneutics and biblical studies. I will explore the text of Jephthah's daughter in Judges 11:29–40. One may be aware that this text is excluded in the Revised Common Lectionary (RCL) that most mainstream Protestant denominations use, which means that it is not preached or read in regular church worship. I argue that the very exclusion of this passage from the lectionary reveals an operative androcentric hermeneutics in liturgy.[2] The exclusion of such a passage in Christian practice serves to veil the violence committed by men

---

2. Procter-Smith, *In Her Own Rite*, 125.

during war in the name of their Gods and silences the voices of women as they mourn and remember. Reading this text as a homiletical theologian, by taking an inter-positioning approach, I will attempt to unsettle androcentric interpretations and reorient us to demonstrate the power of feminist practice as a way of telling and remembering the narrative. In the final section, I intend to lift up the importance of mourning and resistance as communal performance from a Korean cultural and political perspective.

I also adopt an inter-positioning approach pointing to an ethno-specific position of how Korean-Canadian communities converse with and sometimes contests dominant ethno (Europeans) interpretations of the Bible. This essay is indebted to a group of Korean women residing in Canada who gathered and shared their thoughts on the text of Jephthah's daughter in Judges during the retreat in the summer of 2010. They all are ordained ministers from the Presbyterian Church in the Republic of Korea, attend the United Church of Canada as their faith communities, and serve in their local congregations. In this paper, I re-tell our collective wisdom as a way of demonstrating a communal power of sharing experiences and reading the Bible together from a narratival hermeneutical perspective. I will attempt to locate the positions of the daughter and father in the biblical story in light of their sexuality in the context of war while also demonstrating how Korean diaspora women in Canada read this text out of their own social and cultural positions. I will highlight how these women navigate their inter-positioning or "in-between" spaces and identities they inhabit with their narrative agency.

Inter-disciplinary Positioning: Shifting While Sitting

In order for me, a professor of practical theology, to shift from teaching worship and preaching to strictly studying biblical interpretation, I must willingly move beyond my comfort zone (in terms of my academic credentials and personal interests). Practical theologian Joyce Ann Mercer calls the interdisciplinary approach a conundrum, which means it is both a constitutive and an impossible work for practical theologians. Thus it takes humility and vulnerability.[3] While admitting my own feeling of vulnerability in the field of biblical scholarship in silo, I also acknowledge that my position could offer a unique perspective. Elisabeth Schüssler Fiorenza's insight is helpful here. "*Ethos*," she explains, is a word which is rooted in the ancient Greek word, *ethea*, a pedagogical space, where "positionality" becomes critical.[4] Transformation can only happen when education is not only concerned with the formation of the character of persons but also committed to making connections between persons and their place. Thus, here, my interpositional attempt aims at this transformation that can occur when one is committed to making connections between her own subjective position and social location. I propose that the implications of this *ethos* makes senses to Korean-Canadian Christian communities and other diaspora and immigrant communities whose survival often depends on living in-between and shaping hyphenated identities for themselves daily. Our social locations and shifting positions determine how we see the world and shape our actions. As a liturgical and homiletical theologian who has come from Korea and is living as part of the diaspora in Canada, my identity formation must wrestle with this positionality. In this inter-positioning, different threads of identity, race, colonial experience, gender, culture, language, and the Christian Bible are interwoven.[5]

To discuss the importance of interdisciplinary approaches in theological education—especially in practical theology—is nothing new.[6] It is also not new for biblical studies to seek to engage in intertextual interpretation between Old and New Testaments.[7]

3. Mercer, "Interdisciplinarity," 163–89.

4. Schüssler Fiorenza, *Democratizing Biblical Studies*, 164.

5. Trinnh, *Women, Native, Other*, 104

6. See Browning and Reed, *Sacraments*; and Kim-Cragg, *Story and Song*.

7. Mary Ann Beavis illuminates an intertextual relationship between Judges 11:34–40 (LXX) and the story of Jarius's daughter in the synoptic Gospels. See Beavis, "Resurrection," 46–62.

Scholars who proposed minority biblical criticism, for example, also claim that the boundaries of color lines and the barriers between ethnic and racial groups must be overcome. Such efforts also require an "interdisciplinary turn" as an oppositional gesture to dominant criticism. Such an interdisciplinary conversation has brought together *ethnic-relation studies, materialist studies, feminist studies, postcolonial studies, and queer studies.*[8] Much like sitting on a chair with one's legs crossed, such an interdisciplinary positioning approach marks my Korean communities in Canada and, I would argue, contributes to a biblical hermeneutical approach that honors the insights of non-biblical disciplines while reflecting one's own ethno-specific cultural community's ways of engaging the biblical text.

Inter-secting the Text Positioning: Sitting with Others

The story of Jephthah's daughter (Judg 11:34–40) follows the Exodus and conquest of the land of Canaan. In the time of Judges, the Israelites were often oppressed by neighboring nations. Sometimes they were made into slaves (10:7) and because of this were greatly distressed (10:9). Jephthah appears as a mighty warrior in the war against the Ammonites. His goal was to reclaim the land for the Israelites which they had conquered after their escape from Egypt (11:13). It is obvious that territorial conquest was a motivation behind a lot of the military encounters between groups at the time. The gods, be it YHWH, Chemosh, Milcom, or Molech, all played a key role in the war enterprise.[9] Rereading this story requires strategies that deploy interpretative tools to question how the Bible has been used to facilitate, silence, and justify violence, slavery, genocide, and territorial invasion in the name of God or gods.[10] In light of this, let us explore the positions of Jephthah and

---

8. Bailey et al., eds., *They Were All Together*, 35, 27, 28.

9. Dube, *Postcolonial Feminist Interpretation*, 47.

10. Kwok, *Postcolonial Imagination*, 113.

his daughter and how their multiple identities, especially female sexuality and virginity, played a role in this *Theo*-logically charged religious conquest scene.[11]

Is Jephthah a Victim or a Victimizer?

Jephthah spoke about and negotiated with God for the sake of his glory and victory. This eventually led to the death of his daughter. Although the acts of Jephthah are praised elsewhere in the Bible (1 Sam 12:11; Heb 11:32–34), biblical scholars such as Phyllis Trible provide feminist counter-arguments that he was a faithless man who doubted the divine power. She criticizes him as an unfaithful father who caused the death of his only daughter and a selfish man who mourned for himself while blaming her for coming out to meet him.[12] But Jephthah is not the only one criticized. YHWH bears a share of the blame, too. Not only is YHWH silent to Jephthah's vow, YHWH is also silent about the murder of the daughter as a human sacrifice.[13] In this murderous act, the deity is implicated; rhetorically speaking, the narrator of this story is complicit as well. The position of God on this matter is unclear and remains ambiguous.[14]

Whether we blame it on Jephthah's action, YHWH's silence, or even the daughter's non-refusal to fulfill her father's vow, which brought about her doom, female sexuality is an important factor to consider in this text.[15] Jephthah is the son of a prostitute, a condemned and unwanted symbol of female sexuality. This fact about

11. Liew, "Queering Closets," 281.

12. Trible, *Texts of Terror*, 97–109.

13. According to Pseudo-Philo 40:4, the daughter with her companions went down to see the wise men (rather than going to the mountains) to prove her innocence. Yet they were silent, for which God was responsible. See more in Miller, *Tell It On the Mountain*, 117.

14. Exum, "Murder They Wrote," 53.

15. Given that it was customary in Israel at that time for women to come out to greet male warriors upon their return from war and that the daughter would have heard the vow of her father, she might have had the choice not to come out, which she failed to do. See Bohmbach, *Women in Scripture*, 244.

Jephthah's questionable identity leads to such harsh discrimination against him that he is forced to flee his community and live as an outcast (11:3). Trible seems to connect his faithlessness with his family origin: "Jephthah is not Abraham; distrust, not faith . . . [He] is of illegitimate birth; his mother was a harlot."[16] This negative view of Jephthah is the dominant white European male interpretation.[17]

The Korean women group explored the story differently. They wondered if he can also be viewed as a victim of a patriarchal, misogynistic, and hierarchical system. He is a son of a prostitute after all. He is at the edge of society due to his mother's marginalized identity. He comes from a community that is trapped in this inter-tribal relationship of conquest. As a country that was colonized by Japan and is still technically in the midst of a civil war between North and South, the Korean women group sympathized with his conflicted socio-political position, caught in this internal identity tug of war between struggling to reconcile the experiences of being cast out (and then later accepted) by the Israelite elders and his loyalty to his own ethnic and religious group. His decision to fight and vow might have been inspired by the desire to survive, calculated risks in his struggle to move up the social ladder in order to reclaim his dignity, despite his questionable "hybrid" origin and undesirable family background.[18] That he is called to fight by those in power is not about a genuine act of respect or recognition of his strength. Rather, Jephthah is regarded as disposable, a temporary solution to a much more complicated problem. In this sense, he is also a victim.[19]

My Korean group's inter-positioned view of Jephthah is supported by some Jewish feminist biblical scholars. Cheryl Exum

16. Trible, *Texts of Terror*, 101.

17. E.g., the *New Interpreter's Bible*, one of the most popular and widely used commentaries, seems to have such prejudice against him due to his lived experience of being involved in raiding with the outlaws. See Olson, "Book of Judges," 830.

18. Exum, "Tragic Vision and Biblical Narrative," 73.

19. Fewell, "Judges," 76.

critiques Trible's dichotomized view of Jephthah and his daughter as victimizer and victim. She claims that such view echoes a dominant male worldview.[20] Esther Fuchs goes further and insists that he should be considered a victim through his own wrongheaded action. She even refuses to accept his daughter as a victim.[21] These views should not be understood to downplay the violent verbal act committed by Jephthah or to endorse his acts of war and of murder. But the Korean women group and Jewish feminist scholars can tell the story differently. Their narratival agency sheds light on the intersecting positions embedded in this biblical text, which move beyond the sex/gender binary framework, as male oppressor vs. female oppressed.[22] Such a non-dichotomizing reading strategy also moves beyond an anti-sexist rhetoric which sometimes hampers us to see and connect such intersecting issues as economic marginalization, broken families, and war and conquest.[23]

Can Jephthah's Daughter and Korean Women Speak?

My Korean women community in Canada was drawn to Jephthah's daughter, especially her sexuality and her virginity. It was natural for this group to be drawn to her sexuality because they have also seen the ways sexuality is implicated in war, militarism, and colonialism. What is intended here is that the discourse on female sexuality should be positioned as an important intersecting factor, something that the dominant mainstream approach had not fully developed. The group was able to connect this text with the painful stories of Korean comfort women who were forced to become the Japanese-sanctioned prostitutes for male soldiers during the Second World War.[24] The group identified with this

20. Exum, "Murder They Wrote," 60–64.

21. Fuchs, *Sexual Politics*, 178.

22. Our biblical and theological disciplines can learn from Queer studies on this issue. See Butler, *Gender Trouble*.

23. Donaldson, *Decolonizing Feminisms*, 62.

24. A few Korean feminist scholars discuss the comfort women issue in

ancient text because it resonated with the contemporary contexts, where women's sexuality and women's bodies have been used as a weapon or a reward in war and ethnic conflicts. What is intriguing in the story of Jephthah's daughter, however, is the lack of sexual involvement of the men.

The virginity of Jephthah's daughter deserves a closer reading because it heightens the tragedy of her circumstances. That she has never been with a man, never experienced the pleasure of sex, and will never have the fulfillment of motherhood—one of the signs of adulthood in Jewish religious thought—is significant (however problematic this cultural notion for adulthood is for those women who cannot or do not want to have children). At the same time, her virginity symbolizes her innocence and dignity. Perhaps it is for this reason that the honor of her being remembered is granted. The notion of virginity is often used by phallocentric ideology. The untainted female body is deemed the right object for male sexual fantasy and the patriarchal requirement of purity.

Again, the Korean women group contests this notion and tells the story differently. They explored a possibility of the virginity of Jephthah's daughter that may denounce the typical representation of virginity as the perfect female sexuality, as Canadian biblical scholar Peggy Day and Dutch narrative theorist Mieke Bal have explored.[25] The group lifted up the work of several Korean feminists' work on Mariology and the Catholic doctrine of the Immaculate Conception.[26] The group noted that, in light of virginity, there was a parallel between the story of Jephthah's daughter in the

---

light of sexuality, colonialism, and militarism. See Yoo, "Han-Laden Women," 37–46; and Kim, "My/Our Comfort," 75–94.

25. Peggy L. Day reconstructs the meaning of virginity in the case of Jephthah's daughter as a rite of passage for those women who reached puberty and, therefore, able to give birth. See Day, "From the Child," 58–74. Mieke Bal explores the meaning of virginity as nubility or marriageability, arguing against the assumed notion that virginity was most desirable to the men. See Bal, *Death and Dissymmetry*, 47.

26. Han Kuk-Yom claims that Mary's virginity, giving birth to Jesus without depending upon a man, is a "symbol of new humanity" that declares "farewell to patriarchy." See Kuk-Yom, "Mariology as a Base," 238.

Old Testament and the story of Mary in the New Testament. They were able to read inter-textually and to see virginity as a dignified (and divinely inspired) vision of women, free from male control of their own bodies and sexuality. Here, the Korean women group took the inter-positioning approach of reading the Bible in ways that denounce the dominant sexist view of virginity as a symbol of women's virtue and the most desirable condition for men. During the retreat together, our Korean women group approached this aspect of virginity from a perspective that opposes the ideology of purity for the sake of serving men. Instead, they interpreted virginity as a new vision, liberated from the oppression of patriarchy and the violence of war committed by men.

The virginity of Jephthah's daughter points to her young age and poses an interesting juxtaposition to her subsequent speech and action as well as that of her father. According to a narrative literary approach, the daughter's speech and action carry an echo whose memory is sustained by the community through ritual. Jephthah's speech and action, on the other hand, are left unresolved, resulting in consequences for the future that are shallow and empty. Despite her young age, the daughter is responsible for the actions over which she has control and to be respectful of her friends and father.[27] It may be too simplistic to deem her acceptance of death as a totally powerless or submissive act resulting in the perpetuation of a patriarchal hegemony. She presents her father with a bold request.[28] It is significant that this communal act of the women in solidarity with her memory is in stark contrast with the father who had to face his own destiny alone.[29] We turn to this act of solidarity and communal ritual in *memory of her.*

27. Exum, "Murder They Wrote," 62.

28. Harrington, "Pseudo-Philo," 364. According to Pseudo-Philo 40, an anonymous Jewish pseudepigraphical writing based upon an oral narrative tradition in Latin, the daughter is given a name, "Selia." Etymologically, Selia means "requested."

29. Exum, "Tragic Vision and Biblical Narrative," 69, 76–77.

Inter-cultural Positioning:
The Performance of Mourning

The recounting of the story of Jephthah's daughter[30] is a form of celebrating her ability to wield authority over her own life.[31] Such retelling or recounting is not just a verbal act but also an embodied act. It points to a significant liturgical act of women for challenging patriarchy and overcoming violence. Jewish feminist scholar Exum eloquently points out its importance, tapping into a Hebrew word:

> *Ra'yotay*, meaning "my companions," is her last spoken word in the narrative; *'abi*, "my father," was her first. Symbolically, through speech, she journeys from the domain of the father . . . to that of the female companions . . . The resultant image is too powerful to be fully controlled by androcentric interests . . . The ritual of remembrance is conducted by women alone.[32]

The fact that she requests to be away both from her father, who committed the outrageous and irrevocable act of vowing her death, and from the company of men, who continue to unleash war, mass rape, and murder, signifies a break with the culture of violence. It is a critical prophetic desire for the end of patriarchy so that no more violence and unnecessary sacrifice can occur. This request entails awareness, a sense of sisterhood from which new strategies and a vision for the future emerge.[33] Regarding the female communal act of "recounting" (Judg 11:39–40), Canadian feminist biblical scholar Mary Ann Beavis argues that, this act should be understood as countercultural, "a veiled critique of male leadership in Israel" as much as an affirmation of the daughters of

---

30. Fewell argues that this recounting is significant since it occurs only in the other occasion of the song of Deborah (Judg 5:11). See Fewell, *Women's Bible Commentary*, 77.

31. Gerstein, "Ritual Processed," 187.

32. Exum, "Murder They Wrote," 63.

33. Lerner, *Creation of Patriarchy*, 242.

Israel who "play an important, even decisive, role in the life of nation."[34]

Korean feminist biblical scholar Lee Kyung-Sook argues that the intention of the narrator in the text is both to oppose human sacrifice as offering (Lev 18:21; 20:2–5; Deut 12:31; 18:10; Mic 6:7; Jer 7:31; 19:6–15) and to introduce mourning as a communal ritual to be observed (Ezek 8:14; Zech 12:11). It was the women's action of solidarity in the form of mourning—and the act of remembering it—that contributed to ending the inhuman tradition of human sacrificial offering. She compares this biblical narrative with a well-known Korean ancient tale, the story of Emille Bell, by saying that "the sacrifice of a virgin never happened again after this event," in the Korean tale and "So there arose an Israelite custom" (Judg 11:39) in the Hebrew one.[35]

According to legend, the bell was made for a Buddhist temple, but once it was made it did not ring when it was struck. One day, a monk dreamed that if a child was cast into the molten cooper for the bell when it was being made it would ring. So a female child was taken from the village and he had her cast into the red hot metal. When the bell was complete, the bell made the most beautiful sound and echoed with the voice of the young girl calling "emille!"—"mommy!"[36] The Korean group, remembering this story of the Emille bell, were stirred by the conviction that such violent sacrifices of women and children must be stopped. The group shared that we need to create a new story, a counter story, which can embody a restored world. Speaking of embodiment, they recognized the power of the communal ritual, embedded in the story of Jephthah's daughter. They claimed that especially

---

34. Beavis, "Daughter in Israel," 25.

35. Lee, *Women in Hebrew Scripture*, 69–73. She uses a Korean myth called *DaehSaJeChiGeonSuhl*-大蛇際治傳說, which contains a story of a virgin and a toad who was saved by her. When the virgin is offered as a sacrifice to a big snake, the toad sacrifices its life to save her life. The story ends with, "the sacrifice of a virgin never happened again after this."

36. Wikipedia, "Bell of King Seongdeok." In ancient Korea (the sixth century AD), "emille" meant mommy. See also Yonhap News, "History and Legend of Emille Bell."

painful stories must be acted out and communally remembered for healing, for they are too heavy to carry alone.

Here, my Korean women group offers important insights on the meaning of mourning as resistance, involving the act of remembrance for the beloved South Korean president Roh Mu-Hyun, who killed himself. Elsewhere, I have argued that from a Korean cultural and religious perspective, the act of suicide for a cause can be understood as a courageous and concrete act of selfless love for others, not incompatible with the Christian belief in the cross and resurrection of Jesus.[37] The heart of Christian faith lies in the paradox of the resurrection of Jesus Christ, which inevitably required the cross, allowing the cycle of violence to end, with the killing of Jesus in order to save the lives of others for the sake of love. In a similar vein, President Roh said in a final letter he wrote on May 23, 2009, that he was going to kill himself in order to ease the suffering of those who followed him because he loved them.[38] The most remarkable event that followed his death was the innumerable gatherings of Koreans to lament, mourn, and recount his life and death. Millions of Koreans joined in a public act of mourning, crying, singing, standing, and marching together for many months after his death. Herbert Anderson puts such phenomenon this way, "Communal lament for a recognized hero, for example, allows for personal mourning otherwise not permitted . . . Stories of grief demand ritual."[39] Such ritual is personal indeed as an apolitical emotional and cultural act to express one's own sorrow and loss. But it can also become a political act. As Canadian scholar Roger Simon puts it, the act of mourning might have become "a particular form of historiographic *poiesis* . . . an actual making or doing of remembrance . . . performance, elaboration,

37. Kim-Cragg, "Becoming a Feminist Christian," 185–86.

38. Here is my translation of part of his letter: "I owe my life to so many people. I cannot count the suffering that would cause to them because of me. The rest of my life will be nothing but a burden to them . . . Do not be sad. Both life and death are a part of the cycle of nature. Please do not be sorry. Please blame nobody. It is my fate" (*HanKyoReh*, May 24, 2009).

39. Anderson, "Violent Death, Public Tragedy," 189, 191.

interpretation . . . within a space of a community of memory."[40] The act of remembering President Roh as resistance continues to mobilize people beyond the streets of Korea. It has expanded into cyber space, where the Korean diaspora around the globe connect with each other.[41]

It came naturally to our Korean women group to connect the communal ritual in memory of Jephthah's daughter with the communal mourning for the late President Roh since our retreat took place around the first anniversary of his death.[42] From the collective wisdom of our group, we concluded that this ritual of mourning as it happened in Korea and beyond Korea is an inter-cultural, inter-national, and inter-generational event. As a group, we affirmed that the story of Jephthah's daughter and her friends is not just a story of ancient Jewish community but also a story that reflects twenty-first century Korean communities and women around the globe.

Conclusion: From Sitting to Standing

In this essay, I have attempted to assert the importance of inter-positioning as a particular way of reading the Bible which involves an inter-disciplinary, inter-secting, and inter-cultural ethno-specific gesture of relating and crossing. I have also asserted that it is a gesture of negotiation, flexibility, and resistance. The physical and spatial negotiation required to use the Korean sitting position reflects the reality of living in Canada as diaspora of a particular ethnic community.

---

40. Simon, *Touch of the Past*, 153–54.

41. See Rho Mu Hyun Foundation, knowhow.co.kr, and nosamo.org

42. A similar phenomenon took place when the leader and dictator of North Korea, Kim Jeong-il, died on December 17, 2011. A massive, national ritual of public mourning lasted a few weeks. However insane it looks to those of us outside North Korea, the people there told their stories of grief through emotionally charged public mourning—including wailing and excessively displayed bodily acts—to express the loss of their leader.

The story of Jephthah's daughter, excluded from the Revised Common Lectionary, was chosen to showcase an inter-positing reading of the Bible done by a Korean women group living in Canada. The group challenged traditional, androcentric, and dichotomized views of Jephthah and his daughter. As this text was retold by this group, the women reflected on the significance of the communal ritual of mourning among women in solidarity. The group's own narrative ability of interpreting the recent death of the former President Roh helped to deepen insights gleaned from the text.

I have provided a narrative hermeneutics of reading the story of Jephthah and his daughter by describing their inter-positions in terms of intersecting the issues of sexuality, class, militarism, family, politics, and war. Such a reading allows us to move beyond a binary notion of gender, while shedding light upon multiple, complex identities. Furthermore, an inter-positioning reading strategy helps us preach and reflect upon the 21st context of global migration where the realities of living-in-between, border crossing, and boundary transgressing is as common as ever.

Postscript: Narrative of Sitting Continues

I remind myself that I am sitting cross legged on a chair. I have shifted this posture many times while writing. I am reminded that "it is the 'inter'—the cutting edge of translation and negotiation, the *in-between* space—that carries the burden of the meaning of culture."[43] I also feel assured that this burden is not without hope, a spirit that generates energy within, in-between, and beyond. My sitting position will once again be shifted and led by the Spirit which even leads me to stand up in order to assert for myself and others the mutually inclusive and just communities that God so desires.

43. Bhabha, *Location of Culture*, 56.

5

Latinas/os, the Cultural, and the Bible

A Community Finds Itself in the Bible Story

NÉSTOR MEDINA

Introduction

HOW DO DIFFERENT CULTURAL communities engage the biblical text? How do the culturally conditioned faith experiences of entire communities shape their understanding and appropriation of the biblical narrative? And what are some of the insights we can glean from the particular ways in which different cultural communities find and imagine themselves in the biblical narrative? These questions drive my reflections as I seek to understand how Latinas/os in Canada think about the Christian faith and how their own cultural tradition and story impacts and shapes the way they approach and interpret the biblical text. Some of the insights mentioned may apply to Latinas/os in other countries—like the USA—as well, but I wish to focus specifically on how Latina/o Canadians engage the biblical text. Moreover, although I draw heavily on Pentecostal scholarship to bolster my claims on orality, I believe the insights I describe here are useful for thinking about how Latina/o Canadians in general interact with the biblical text.

Hermeneutics is my central focus: I propose that Latinas/os find in their lived-faith and lived-experiences the hermeneutical rubric for "reading" and "interpreting" their own story in the biblical narrative. Moving beyond a "literalist" reading of the Bible, Latina/o Canadians enter into a complex dialogical relation with the biblical narrative. The impact and conditioning character of their cultural traditions as experienced in daily life induce them to find themselves in the biblical narrative. In other words, I suggest that Latina/o Canadians, in their multiple cultural expressions and traditions, display what I call *lived hermeneutics*. That is, a composite of interpretive dialogical relations in which their everyday lives and narratives as people shape and inform the way they understand and interpret the Bible. This lived hermeneutics constitutes the first three sections of the paper. In a fourth brief section, I draw some important implications for the field of hermeneutics noting some of the various ways in which Latina/o Canadians engage the Bible collectively. My intention is to show how "orality" plays a central role among Latina/o Canadian biblical hermeneutics. As such, it should be considered an important feature for interpreting the Bible narrative.

The Latina/o Everyday Experience

Latina/o Canadians are relatively new to the Canadian context.[1] For example, there are some marked differences between Latinas/

1. The number of Latin American immigrants in Canada has almost doubled between 1990 and 2001 to 520,260. It has grown exponentially since 2001, but the numbers registered in more recent census statistics have not changed significantly. It is important, however, to note that three out of every five Latinos/as reside in Toronto, Montreal, and Vancouver. Strictly speaking, Latin American immigration began strongly in the 1970s and has continued for the three last decades. Although there was a "Lead Wave" in 1956–1965 (1965–1969 for South American people), and more recently, in the 1990s, a wave of professional skilled workers and business class, the bulk of the immigrant population came to Canada during the three last decades of the twentieth century. For a detailed discussion of the various migratory patterns and present conditions of Latina/o immigrants in Canada, see Ginieniewicz, "Political Participation in Canada," 34–35; Szmulewicz et al., "How is Canada

os in the USA and Latina/o Canadians. US Latinas/os exist in liminal social spaces where they are simultaneously "American" but never fully welcome. The anti-immigration and anti-immigrant sentiments in the present US administration are a good example of how many people still think of Latinas/os as foreigners, immigrants, or illegals, despite the fact that the majority of Latinas/os were born in the USA. In Canada, Latinas/os still view themselves (and are generally viewed) as immigrants. In both contexts, though the experiences are different, Latinas/os face discrimination and marginalization as part of their everyday life. Hence, the experiences of immigration, marginalization, discrimination, and poverty shape Latina/o Canadian self-understanding as people and impact the way they look toward the Bible to find meaning in their lives. In Latina/o hermeneutics, these motifs and themes appear again and again in reflections and are embodied in daily activities, all articulated within the frame of God's salvation.[2]

The Impact of Latina/o Canadian Culture and Experience

The biblical story of divine redemption—in its spiritual, social, and economic senses—captivates Latina/o Canadian Christians and is part of their interpretive frame. In other words, they approach the Bible with the expectation that, within its narrative, believers encounter the divine salvific promise and can imagine its actualization in their life-situations and immediate context. It gives them hope. When they read the events and miracles that take

---

Looking." For a brief analysis of the challenges migrant workers face, see Hinnenkamp, "Justicia for Migrant Workers," 148–53. Of the Latina/o population, those of Mexican heritage account for 15 percent, those from Chile are 14 percent, and Salvadorean are 11 percent. Latinas/os are primarily concentrated in the four provinces of Quebec (27 percent), Ontario (47 percent), Alberta (9 percent), and British Columbia (17 percent) with small groups in Manitoba. In Quebec, Latinas/os are overrepresented, accounting for 20 percent of Quebec's population. See Statistics Canada, "Latin American Community in Canada."

2. Medina, "Being Church as Latina/o Pentecostals."

place in the Bible, they simply are convinced that if it happened in the Bible, it can happen to us now!

Latina/o Canadian hermeneutics is a dynamic back-and-forth interweaving of the messy and difficult reality of daily life, individual experience, cultural traditions, and the reading of the biblical text. They move from a literal reading and interpretation of the text to a merging of their own story with the biblical story. These hermeneutics are not only or merely cognitive engagements, they are part of the larger interlacing of context, community, cultural tradition, and the Bible as people live their day-to-day faith. These are also not abstract categories: Latina/o Canadians live their faith as Latinas/os in a context of great social inhospitability, under enormous cultural pressure by a dominant culture, and, at the same time, with rich, promising possibilities of having a better life than the life they left behind in their birth countries. Many Latinas/os have to struggle to make ends meet. Many risk their lives crossing the border. Others migrate with some financial resources, seeking to integrate in the Canadian social fabric. Still others feel the need to overstay their visas only to be stigmatized as foreigners or illegals.[3] There is much more that can be said about the precarious conditions in which many immigrants live in Canada.[4] For now, I simply wish to focus on the fact that Latina/o Canadians draw on the biblical text for inspiration and insight in order to understand their living situation and to find hope as they confront

3. Those people who choose to stay in Canada without regularizing their documents are condemned to suffer surveillance and the constant threat of deportation. Most of them work to survive, and some work two jobs or more to make ends meet. They pay their taxes, yet they are often exploited; there are no social mechanisms for their protection as well as no access to services such as health care. Moreover, although the government is aware of their precarious condition, it does not want to create ways for them to regularize their status in the country. The psychological effects of living under these circumstances are traumatic. See Saad, "Cost of Invisibility," 137–54; and Jiménez, "Ottawa rules Out Amnesty." Estimates range between 35,000 to 120,000 people who live without regularized documentation in Canada. Prior to 1947, there was no such thing as a legal or illegal Canadian citizen.

4. For a discussion on how Canada has historically dealt with immigrants see Medina, "Reflections of a Snow Mexican."

their new social and political context. As they come together as believing communities, they draw on the biblical text and engage in a complex and dynamic exercise of collective cultural memory and spiritual discernment.

At a basic level, one can say that Latina/o Canadians are literalists because they believe that what is written in the Bible happened the way it is described. In this sense, they are strongly modernist—influenced by the legacy of foreign missionaries and theologies—because they ascribe to strict readings of events as narrated. However, to conclude that literalism is a totally accurate description of the ways in which Latina/o Canadians approach the text would foreclose the debate prematurely. Such an affirmation is too simplistic a description of Latina/o Canadian hermeneutics; it is a caricature of the complex ways in which Latina/o Canadians engage, use, and talk about the biblical text.

Admittedly, there is an operative literalist tendency that, in some communities, has produced rigid readings of the Bible from which strict ethical and social principles have been developed. This rigidness often corresponds with people's cultural backgrounds. For example, Latina/o Canadians welcome Paul's exhortation for children to honor their parents in Ephesians 6:2 because respect for the elderly and one's parents is already a generally accepted cultural value. In the same way, many Latina/o Canadians find an affinity with Ephesians 5:22–33 (and other passages where women are told to submit to their husbands), because they have inherited patriarchal structures in their cultures. I would argue, however, that such readings constitute a "first level" surface reading. As I have explained elsewhere, when Latinas/os arrive to Canada (or the USA, for that matter) and begin to incorporate into the Canadian social fabric, their own cultural traditions begin to change—just as their presence changes the Canadian cultural milieu.[5] Most Latina/o Canadians outgrow this "first level" hermeneutics and begin to reconfigure earlier, literalist interpretations of the Bible on the ground. Their internal community and family dynamics change, giving way to new, more sophisticated dynamics

5. Medina, "Being Church as Latina/o Pentecostals."

and understandings of the biblical text, though sometimes they reproduce the literalist discourse in public.

The interweaving between Latina/o Canadian cultural traditions and biblical interpretation can also be seen in the ways in which certain culturally laden notions that resonate with the biblical text broaden Latina/o theological understandings. For example, Latina/o Canadians claim for themselves the promise in Acts: "Believe in the Lord Jesus Christ and you and your family will be saved" (Acts 16:31). Consequently, they have the theological expectation that one's personal salvation is bound up with the salvation of one's entire family. The emphasis on family carries specific cultural overtones, but it is here where the Latina/o Canadian cultural understanding of family and the biblical notion of church merge. There is a convergence between the Latina/o conception of family, the development and celebration of familial ties, and entrance into the community of believers by way of conversion. The cultural importance of family plays out because of the significance given to the community of believers as extended family.[6] Thus, becoming a member of a church community carries the added meaning of entering into the larger family of God. The dynamic interrelation between the individual, the community, and the family reflects a specific Latina/o Canadian cultural ethos and functions in relation to crucial aspects of their own sense of identity in the existing social climate of discrimination and marginalization, all the while redefining the theological understanding of the *ekklesía*. In this dynamic interchange, we can already see that Latina/o Canadians overcome a literalist reading of the biblical text.

Latina/o Canadian Lived Hermeneutics

I was taught that the Bible story included my own story. I was also taught that the Bible was not a book to be "read." The act of "reading"

6. Discussing the connection between worship, community, and family, González describes family as a "rather . . . vast assemblage of people who are related in a multiplicity of ways so that they have a sense of belonging, but not necessarily excluding others" (González, "Worship and Fiesta," 256).

the biblical text is something that had to be done in conversation with the members of my faith community. Many Latina/o Canadians see reading the biblical text as a communal rather than an individual process. But reading the Bible in community also means at least three important things: (1) It means reading with those who share the faith. Strong communal ties are crucial both culturally and theologically. (2) It means engaging the text with those who know and can identify with one's experience of discrimination, marginalization, poverty, racism, and immigration. As a community of faith, there is a history, a set of existential experiences that deeply shape how the text is read and interpreted. And (3) it means reading the text with one's newly acquired family. The interconnection between the cultural dimension, the experiences of people, and a shared reading of the text brings about new levels of intimacy that can only be defined as "familial ties."[7]

I argue, therefore, that the connection between the personal and the community has important hermeneutical implications. As Latina/o Canadians relate to and engage the Scripture, they enter a "second level" hermeneutics in which they believe that their story is part of the larger divine scheme. That means that they do not only read the Bible to find the story of Israel. The meaning of the text is perceived to be in a dialogical tension between the semantic horizon of the text and the existential horizon of the believer and their community.[8] Believers actually find themselves in the Bible story; the Bible story is their own story.

---

7. These "familial ties" are very fluid and make it possible for many Latinas/os who are alone in the country to find a group of people with whom to share their lives in Canada. In this sense, the familial ties cross-cultural boundaries among Latinas/os, say between Mexicans and Argentinians, Salvadorans and Peruvians, or Guatemalans and Colombians. There are shared cultural factors that allow for these intercultural engagements. The familial ties, of course, are negotiated constantly because of questions of language, class, education, perceived racialized issues, and place/country of origin. At the same time, these factors make it really difficult for Latina/o Canadians to extend the familial ties to other non-Latina/o or non-Latin American ethnocultural groups.

8. I am borrowing here from what Hans-Georg Gadamer called "fusion of horizons." See Gadamer, *Truth and Method.*

Latina/o Canadians are not naïve. They recognize that the reality of believers here and now differs greatly from the reality described in the Bible; they know they are not living in biblical times. Rather, engaging the biblical narrative and rehearsing the stories of Bible characters in their own lives helps give significance to their own faith journey. Stated differently, the unique context of Latina/o Canadians shapes how they approach the text, the kinds of questions they ask from the text, and the kinds of answers they find in the text. In the hermeneutical moment, Latina/o Canadians' cultural traditions, socio-cultural context, broad sense of community, and interaction with Bible are woven together. In a sense, if God was active in the biblical stories, then God is understood to be active now among them and for them. For those who are often pushed to the social periphery, made socially undesirable, criticized culturally, are generally unwelcome, and among whom many are criminalized for not having proper documentation, the discovery of their story in the biblical text is powerfully transformative.

Latina/o Canadians, Orality, and Biblical Interpretation

To repeat, for Latina/o Canadians, the biblical text is not understood to be designed for individual "consumption." In the same way, Latina/o Canadian hermeneutics is not the result of intellectual exchanges in light of a written text. Borrowing from Jacques Derrida, this hermeneutic is not a logocentrism. Rather, it takes place at the dialogical level of orality.[9] In other words, if you want to know how Latina/o Canadians interpret and engage the Bible, then hear their songs, listen to their stories and testimonies, and pay attention to the content of their prayers and their sermons (*testimonios, coros, oraciones, y predicaciones*). My intention is not to romanticize these practices as if they contain no aspects that can

---

9. For a fuller discussion on the intersection between the cultural dimension, context, and hermeneutics, see Medina, "Orality and Context," 97–123.

be engaged critically. I am simply highlighting their rich herme-neutical import and theological content.[10]

The oral character of Latina/o Canadians is rapidly changing because of the influx of immigrants from Latin America with high levels of institutional education. Still, it is precisely the oral nature of their faith traditions and expressions that have contributed to the preservation of its dynamism over the years. Orality continues to shape and inform Latina/o Canadians liturgical rituals, practic-es, and beliefs; it is the means through which the next generation of Latina/o Canadians are socialized into the Christian faith and learn to encounter God in the biblical text.

Hermeneutically speaking, the oral dimension creates a context of "epistemological fluidity" and inclusion by which other forms of knowledge from institutional training, for instance, are also welcome. As José Míguez Bonino states, what is emphasized is the "freedom of the Spirit."[11] Stated differently, the "symbolic universe" of the community's wisdom, life experiences, testimo-nies, practices, and rituals become the coherent cosmovision and interpretive framework for understanding and interpreting the world, God's activity within it (through the Spirit), and the biblical text. In other words, orality is an epistemological source, a way of knowing and living.[12] More pertinent to hermeneutics:

10. Here I am in agreement with Bernardo Campos. Although he speaks specifically of Latin American Pentecostals, I believe his insights apply to Latina/o Canadians as well. I, too, argue that the lack of explicit written theological material does not indicate a lack of an intellectual organizing of beliefs. Theology cannot be and is not expressed only by those who articulate it "systematically" and in written form. If by "systematic" we understand the arbitrary "freezing of a body of doctrine in a theological system more or less coherent within itself and with the group in power," then Latina/o Canadians are asystematic. But if by systematization we understand "a methodological process through which the subject people-church reflect upon its action and organizes it in a coherent whole with its own interests," such a notion no longer makes any sense—because people's lives or Christian living is neither "coher-ent," "consistent," or sanitized. Christian life and Christian living are messy, painful, and full of contradictions. See Campos, "Lo testimonial," 133.

11. Míguez Bonino, *Rostros del protestantismo latinoamericano*, 76.

12. Campos, "Lo testimonial," 129.

orality emphasizes the manifestation of different patterns of understanding, knowledge creation, and interaction with reality and the world as narrated by the biblical text. Undisturbed by the critical concerns of modernity, orality points to the eruption of different epistemological networks and forms of knowing, which fall within the sphere of the "pre-critical, and have thus far been dismissed by academia."[13]

The convergence between the biblical story and the Latina/o Canadian experience takes on a life of its own that is irreducible to written formulae, established canons of theological knowledge, and conventional rules of biblical interpretation.[14]

In some other contexts, orality has been understood as a means by which the popular masses resist and subvert official codes and dominant standards of theological production.[15] Yet, as I see it, orality among Latina/o Canadians goes beyond resistance and subversion. In terms of hermeneutics, I would argue that orality among Latina/o Canadians points to the complex life networks, rituals, and practices by which they construct theological knowledge and actualize the meaning of the biblical text for their immediate context and experience.

Walter Hollenweger argues that to reject the rich theological content of orality would be tantamount to denying the entire background and historical ground upon which the Bible is based.[16] For Latinas/os, these culturally conditioned oral expressions and

13. Medina, "Orality and Context," 114.

14. Walter Hollenweger is correct when he muses that one of the greatest future challenges Christianity will face will be the dialogue between the representatives of written theology and those of oral theology. According to him, part of the problem lies in the fact that a good portion of the representatives of the oral theology are poor and of "color," while those of the written theology have great financial means and are "white." See Hollenweger, *El pentecostalismo*, 479.

15. This dynamic is identified among Pentecostals and Ecclesial Base Communities in Latin America. See Sepúlveda, "Pentecostalism as Popular Religiosity," 88; Álvarez, "Lo popular," 89–100; and Lai, "Andragogy of the Oppressed."

16. Hollenweger, *El pentecostalismo*, 479.

practices put their hermeneutical collective memory on display. I affirm the oral character of Latina/o Canadian hermeneutics to reiterate the close interconnection between the cultural dimension and biblical hermeneutics. Indeed, it is common knowledge that orality plays a central role in the transmission of Christian teachings, especially in the worship service or the liturgical sphere.[17] However, my attention to Latina/o Canadian orality does not so much correspond with the place of orality in the liturgical sphere as it does with the fact that orality itself (along with worship, to some extent) has remained absent from hermeneutical discussions.

I wish to emphasize the hermeneutical importance of orality. As constitutive of Latina/o Canadian oral tradition, songs and music, liturgy, narrative, dreams, and visions play a crucial role in the hermeneutical task. These practices constitute *other* modes of doing hermeneutics (and theology); the meaning of the text is not reduced to or expressed in "systematic," written articulations. Bonino reminds us again that, in Latin American (and Latina/o) orality, we find the community's "implicit theology"[18] and—I would add—the least sanitized interpretations of the biblical text.

The lack of explicit, written theological hermeneutics must not be mistaken for a lack of the intellectual organizing of beliefs among Latina/o Canadians. Orality encompasses different processes and lines of engagement with the biblical text that are irreducible to textual analysis and engagement. People's experiences draw meaning from the text that is not available by way of textual analysis alone. According to Wolfgang Vondey, orality places the emphasis on the memory of human experience, the story line, the characters, and the transformative power of the Word of God rather than on the story, structure, textuality, rhetoric, historicity, or form of the biblical texts.[19] In other words, it is in these complex and dynamic interactions between context, cultural tradition, individual participation, and community that Latina/o Canadians

---

17. Archer, *Pentecostal Hermeneutic*, 106; and Neumann, *Pentecostal Experience*, 111.

18. Míguez Bonino, *Rostros del protestantismo latinoamericano*, 75.

19. Vondey, *Beyond Pentecostalism*, 61.

are able to read and interpret the biblical text and encounter the divine disclosure within it. Such a dynamic interaction takes place as they go out into the streets and experience the stigma of being seen as foreigners, as they seek employment, as they are stopped by the police—who stereotype them as drug-traffickers or gang members—or as they struggle to avoid deportation, barely earning enough money to send to family members back in their birth countries. Their hermeneutic is intimately connected to their very real, day-to-day material context and lived experiences.

6

Bhakti, Sadhu Sundar Singh, and the Art of Reading Scripture

An Indian Approach to Reading the Bible in Canada

ALISON HARI-SINGH

Introduction

I WAS BORN WITH my feet in two worlds. One foot was rooted in the paradigms and ethos of the place I was raised while the other was ineluctably coupled with the cultural history and genetic pull of my ethnic heritage. Both my father and mother hail from North India—Himachel Pradesh and Punjab, respectively—but in 1968, only a few months into their marriage, they immigrated to the United Kingdom. In 1982, due to persistent social unrest, they decided to relocate again, this time with two young children in tow, from England to Canada, under the banner of "Canadian multiculturalism"—the notion that those new to Canada could maintain their ethnic heritage and still be fully-fledged Canadians. Nonetheless, growing up in northern Saskatchewan, everything around me said that the narratives, ways of thinking, and practices of European settlers were normative—not simply for white Canadians but for all people, regardless of race, culture, and ethnicity.[1]

As a child, the solution to my "identity issues" was to reject being Indian and fully embrace being Canadian, which really meant adopting a white Canadian way of being. The fact that my parents were (and still are) practicing Christians merely compounded my angst. For my parents, being Indian and being Christian are not mutually exclusive identities. In the world in which they encountered Christianity—that of the English and US missionary schools long-established in Northern India—there existed an already developed Indian-Christian metaphysics. This was not the case in rural Saskatchewan. In that context, being Christian meant *not* being Indian. I had to choose, so I did.

Some thirty years later, I still find myself choosing. But, in many ways, the act of choosing has become even more challenging. Today, I see myself as a Christian who is both Indian and Canadian, someone whose thinking has been shaped by the values, practices, and ways of thinking of the Indian diaspora *as well as* the North Atlantic. Neither of these particular cultural identities supersedes the other. Instead, I understand my identity to be hybrid and heterogeneous.[2] In more recent years, this hybrid identity has been reshaped by a conscious retrieval of "Indian-ness." However, the reclamation of my Indian identity has less to do with going back to India. Instead, I am interested in understanding how being Indian allows me to live an authentic Christian life here in Canada.

The following is my attempt at articulating my ethno-cultural identity as it pertains to being a South Asian immigrant engaged in a particular Christian practice—namely, reading the Bible in Canada. Accordingly, there are two serious issues at stake: (1) What does it mean to be a Christian if you are not of European descent? (2) What

1. This paper is a springboard from my reading of Malhotra, *Being Different*. More importantly, it is a theological reflection on the stories of personal encounter with Sadhu Sundar Singh and his spiritual legacy as handed down to me from my father's side of the family.

2. Some scholars consider the term "hybridity" problematic: Parry, "Problems in Current Theories"; Young, *White Mythologies*; Mitchell, "Different Diasporas," 533–53; and Werbner "Multiple Identities."

does it mean to be a Christian if you are not of European descent and reside in a country shaped by the norms, values, and epistemologies of the North Atlantic? The common practice I have observed within my own family and among other Indo-Canadian Christians is that while they do attend established Christian churches, they more often gather together in their own independent Indian churches. These are spaces in which they can speak their own language, sing their own songs, and express Christian belief and practice in an Indian way. In other words, even though they are Christians, they are reluctant to give up their cultural commitments. They do not feel obligated, necessarily, to take on European assumptions and ways of thinking when it comes to considerations of Christian faith and practice. Christianity, for them, is not a European religion. Hence, European understandings of Christian belief and practice do not define what is legitimate.

This paper unearths a source from which Indo-Canadian Christians might draw in order to articulate how they read the Bible: the life and thought of the Indian Christian mystic Sadhu Sundar Singh. Singh's theologically and culturally expressed life of *bhakti* was the cornerstone of his Christian faith and practice. Moreover, *bhakti* shaped how he approached reading Christian Scripture. His example serves as an archetypal form of discipleship that many North Indian Christians living in Canada today emulate. I contend, therefore, that by examining the life and thought of Sadhu Sundar Singh, an analogous Indo-Canadian Christian hermeneutic is uncovered. This hermeneutic demonstrates how many Indian Christians read the Bible in the Canadian context in a way that is Christian, Indian, and not defined by European standards of methodological legitimacy.

In order to demonstrate this thesis, I first explore the Hindu notion of *bhakti*. I then provide a brief biography of Sadhu Sundar Singh's life. Next, I explore the theological concepts and methods that underscore Singh's Christian *bhakti*. Finally, based on Singh's methodological approach, I offer a two-pronged framework for Indian Christians living in Canada, who, like myself, are reluctant to leave Christian faith and the art (or skill) of reading Scripture to the domain of European understandings of Christianity. My hope is that this Indian approach to reading the Bible might be a methodology all Canadians can access and practice.

Bhakti Defined

In order to argue my case—that an examination of the Christian *bhakti* of Sadhu Sundar Singh denotes a heuristic hermeneutic by which many Indian Christians read the Bible in Canada—the term *bhakti* must be defined. Defining *bhakti*, however, necessitates two steps. First, I provide a very rough outline of Hindu theological[3] conceptions of cosmology and ontology. Second, I establish a working definition of *bhakti* that relates Singh's Christian *bhakti* to the wider Hindu tradition.

Hindu Theology: Cosmology, Ontology, and Revelation

It is difficult to enter a discussion regarding the nature of *bhakti* without providing some context. *Bhakti* is not a silo concept; it is couched in an entire cosmology and system of thought. As Hillary Rodrigues points out, there is neither a single, authoritative Hindu cosmology nor is there a singular Hindu theology. Nonetheless, Hindu cosmology, whether theological or philosophical, is essentially cyclical. Hindus believe that both time and creation move in repetitive cycles of rebirth (*samsara*). These cycles are not necessarily a renewal. Rather, creation moves toward degeneration over time based on the principle of *karma*. *Karma* is a moral principle of causality in which good deeds (*punya*) are commendable while wrong deeds (*papa*) have negative consequences. All created things are caught up in these repetitive cycles of *samsara* and are

---

3. "Theology," here, refers more broadly to the cosmological arguments that make up Hindu religious belief. Hindu theology is, essentially, theistic, while Hindu philosophy is atheistic. See Flood, *Introduction to Hinduism*, 224.

ultimately seeking *moksha* (ultimate release, liberation, or salvation from *samsara*).[4]

Hinduism is more than a sensibility. It is a complex system of beliefs founded on the written texts believed to be revelatory, particularly the Vedas.[5] Although there are many Hindu schools of thought and theology, one Hindu philosopher, Shankara, has become the most highly regarded over the centuries. Shankara was a high caste Hindu—a Brahmin—from South India who lived during the eighth or ninth century AD. He is thought to have founded the *matha* or monastic practice within Hinduism. Accordingly, Shankara did not marry but lived the life of a *samnyasin*[6]—a solitary wandering monk.

Shankara's philosophical theology is known as Advaita Vedanta. It is based on a notion of radical non-dualism.[7] For Shankara, only one thing is absolutely real—Brahman—and Brahman is indivisible.[8] Since Brahman cannot be divided into constitutive parts, consequently, *atman*—the human being's true Self—must be identical with Brahman.[9] When one realizes that Brahman is "all there is,"[10] and that one's true nature is Brahman, the human being is liberated both bodily and spiritually.

For Shankara, any conception, thought, or imagining we have about Brahman, is essentially the work of *maya* (illusion or ignorance). When we apply such attributes to Brahman, we reduce Brahman to an ultimate deity or "Lord." The Lord (*Ishvara*) is the

4. Rodrigues, *Introducing Hinduism*, 53.

5. Sharma, "Hinduism," 26.

6. Rodrigues, *Introducing Hinduism*, 250.

7. Advaita Vedanta is reluctant to impose any quality upon Brahman, thus, it engages in a process of negation called *neti neti*, meaning Brahman is "neither this, nor that." See Rodrigues, *Introducing Hinduism*, 251. Similar to apophatic theology in Eastern Orthodoxy, it is an analytical process of conceptualizing an idea or thing by defining what it is not.

8. Rodrigues, *Introducing Hinduism*, 250. This tradition of radical non-dualism or absolute monism upholds the belief of the Reality of the one over that of the many. See Flood, *Introduction to Hinduism*, 239.

9. Flood, *Introduction to Hinduism*, 241.

10. Rodrigues, *Introducing Hinduism*, 250.

one who presides over the world and is the object of religious devotion. *Bhakti* is utter commitment and devotion to *Ishvara*. Shankara sees such commitment to *Ishvara* as permissible but at a lower level of knowledge of Brahman. It is a remnant of ignorance which one hopes eventually to transcend fully.[11] Thus, in Shankara's philosophical theology, whenever particular qualities or characteristics are projected upon Brahman, there remains a vestige of *maya*,[12] and *moksha* has not been obtained.

The Origin and Meaning of *Bhakti*

The Vedanta of Shankara is arguably the standard interpretation of Hindu philosophical theology. Around the first or second century AD, however, a form of popular Hinduism—*bhakti*—emerged based on a novel interpretation of the Bhagavad Gita.[13] The practices of this new movement centered on devotion to the personal deities of Vishnu, Shiva, and Dev through icons, shrines, temples, holy men, devotional songs, dances, religious drama, festivals, and pilgrimage. Through *bhakti*, Vedic religion—which was mainly sacrificial and aniconic—became tangibly connected to popular practices of devotion, icons, and "foreign" participation.[14] These newfound devotional practices preserved the Vedic tradition, yet acknowledged and gave a legitimate place to popular religious practice.

Bhakti Hinduism, contrary to traditional Hindu teaching, gave central prominence to devotion toward a deity as a means to *moksha*. Although "not everyone can be a priest or a learned seer . . . everyone can know the Lord through devotion and can

11. Flood, *Introduction to Hinduism*, 241–42.

12. Rodrigues, *Introducing Hinduism*, 251.

13. Karen Prentiss notes that the emergence of the *bhakti* movement in the first and second centuries AD was essentially a reform movement within Hinduism. Moreover, it was something like the Protestant movement in Christian Europe in terms of why it emerged; that is, as a reform to over-indulgence within the tradition. See Prentiss, *Embodiment of Bhakti*, 5.

14. Hopkins, "Bhakti Hinduism," 99.

perform his duties as a form of devotion to him."[15] Thus, for those without social standing in Hindu society, *bhakti* Hinduism provided a way to participate fully in religious life.

If this is the case, what does *bhakti* look like? Chhaganlal Lala highlights five essential prerequisites of *bhakti*: human birth, high aspiration, faith, surrender, and prayer. All who are born human possess the condition of higher aspiration, but we squander this objective on transient things. Thus, the only way for the human being to overcome this tendency and surrender to the Lord completely is through faith. Surrender is the dedication of one's whole being, body, mind, and action to the Lord, but faith is the anchor. With faith comes surrender; by surrendering to the Lord, a person can attain *moksha* in one single life. Finally, a faith-filled and surrendered soul always senses the presence of God through prayer. Prayer is the means by which the devotee communes with the Lord and, thereby, receives the grace of God.[16]

Such recompense is not realized in a vacuum, however. There are aids to *bhakti*. The first is *satsanga*, or holy company, and the second is holy reading.[17] Of the two, knowledge of Scripture is of utmost importance because it is the only authority by which one decides the courses of action and inaction. Moreover, Scripture reveals truth to us. As Lala puts it, by reading we "seek the treasure . . . the Lord himself."[18] Yet, while reading Scripture and *satsanga* are aids to *bhakti*, they are not ends in themselves. Reading, regardless of how helpful and revelatory it is, is not the final goal. In other words, time with Scripture alone can never substitute one's simple and direct experience of God through prayer. Nor can it provide greater spiritual insights than those accrued in unsurpassable moments of worship.[19] Thus, it is in the observance of prayer

---

15. Hopkins, "Bhakti Hinduism," 99.

16. Lala, *Philosophy of Bhakti*.

17. Lala, *Philosophy of Bhakti*, 135.

18. Lala, *Philosophy of Bhakti*, 139.

19. Lala, *Philosophy of Bhakti*, 139–40.

and devout worship that the human being ultimately encounters God[20] in all God's grace and glory.

Sadhu Sundar Singh and the *Bhakti* Tradition

As stated earlier, the *bhakti* tradition within Hinduism evolved due to popular practices already in existence. However, *bhakti* Hinduism also developed because Hindu theologians took issue with certain philosophical assertions within the standard tradition. An eleventh-century Hindu theologian named Ramanuja, for example, contested Shankara's impersonal Absolute Reality (*nirguna Brahman*) as a "useless God."[21] Instead, Ramanuja argued for some form of Divine transcendence and, thus, a separation of matter from transcendent reality.

The assertion of this basic division between the Divine and the material radically changed the direction of Hindu belief and practice all over India. Not surprisingly, Christianity, a religion that maintains a similar tenet, took root in those parts of India in which there was already a strong *bhakti* tradition. Through *bhakti*, the *bhakta* could become a Christian and yet not feel that they had left their Indian way of being behind.[22] *Bhakti* Hinduism was the spiritual tradition in which Sadhu Sundar Singh was formed, the tradition in which he realized his own form of Christian *bhakti*.

The following section begins with a brief biography of Singh's life. I then highlight those aspects that constitute Singh's Christian *bhakti*. Finally, I look at how Christian *bhakti*, as Singh understood it, influenced the way he read Christian Scripture, thus demonstrating that Singh's Christian *bhakti* serves as an archetypal example by which many Indians practice reading the Bible in a Canadian context.

---

20. The reference to "God" here is not to a monotheistic supernatural being, but to transcendent Reality or Brahman.

21. Boyd, *Indian Christian Theology*, 111.

22. Boyd, *Indian Christian Theology*, 111–12.

Singh's Biography in Brief

Sundar Singh was born on September 3, 1889, in the village of Rampur in Punjab, India. He came from an affluent family who, though they were devout Sikhs, made sure their son was also educated in the essential teachings of the Hindu *bhakti* tradition.[23] Singh was an earnest child with a receptive conscience. He was also zealous in his convictions. His conversion story is a case in point: after the devastating deaths of his mother and brother, Sundar's father sent him to the local primary school, run by the American Presbyterian Mission in his village. Singh hated Christianity and refused to read the daily Bible lesson. In his later life, Singh admitted of his childhood days that while the Gospel teaching of the love of God attracted him, he still thought it was false and therefore opposed it.[24] He was so staunch in his opinion that one day, in a zealous rage, he tore up a New Testament and burned it in the presence of others, including his father. His actions burdened him so terribly with guilt that he cried out to God in prayer asking for God to be revealed. If God did not answer, Singh confessed that he would have gone down to the railway and committed suicide.

Singh received his answer, though it was not what he expected. In this moment of prayerful desperation, he waited for Krishna or Buddha or some other *avatar* of Hinduism, but none appeared. There was, however, a light that began to shine in his room. The light hovered and grew in intensity. Within it was none other than the living Christ—the one he thought was dead. Christ asked him, "Why do you persecute me? See, I have died on the cross for you and for the whole world." Singh wrote: "These words were burned into my heart as by lightning, and I fell on the ground before him. My heart was filled with inexpressible joy and peace, and my whole life was entirely changed."[25]

---

23. Boyd, *Indian Christian Theology*, 92.

24. Charles Moore notes that Singh opposed colonial religion. See his introduction in *Essential Writings*.

25. Appasamy, *Sundar Singh*, 21.

Eventually, Singh's conversion created such a rift between him and his father that he was "disowned" and cast out of his family's home. Missionaries in the area took pity and sent him to finish his schooling. On September 3, 1905, Singh received the sacrament of baptism from a clergy person working with the Church Missionary Society in Simla. He was 16 years old. A month later, barely a grown man, Singh appeared in the wooded hills of Sabathu in the saffron-colored robes of a sadhu.[26]

The rest of Singh's life would be marked by travel. Though he never completed a seminary degree, Singh lived the life of an itinerant mystic evangelist. His evangelistic work took him all over India and even into Tibet. Stories of his travels became so renown that he was asked to go on speaking tours in Europe—where he had become a controversial figure[27]—Southeast Asia, and the USA. In due course, the constant travel took a toll on Singh's health. He could no longer go on speaking tours, but Christian publishers began requesting written works. Subsequently, in the last few years of his life, he published eight small books. These were written mainly in Urdu and translated into English, French, German, Swedish, Japanese, Mandarin, and every other prominent dialect in the subcontinent. Writing, however, was not enough for him. He longed to see Tibet converted to Jesus Christ. In 1929, at the age of 39, Singh set out for Tibet from his Sabathu home and was never heard from or seen again.

Singh's Christian *Bhakti*

It is clear that Singh's writings and lectures reveal an inherently "inculturated" faith.[28] As Streeter and Appasamy note, Singh did

26. Moore, *Essential Writings*, 17–18.

27. Moore, *Essential Writings*, 25. In the 1920s, Singh became such a controversial figure that arguments about him were called the *Sadhustreit* ("Sadhu fight") in German Roman Catholic circles.

28. By "inculturation" I mean the adaptation (or translation) of Christian teachings to a particular cultural tradition and the subsequent development, or even reinterpretation, of Christian teachings due to the influence of that

not deliberately set out to "Indianize" Christianity. Rather, for him, the Gospel message is *supra* national. Singh was a man who was "truly Indian in all his ways and thoughts," and yet, he had entered fully "into the heart of the Gospel," not into "the Christian tradition of the West."[29] As Singh himself said, "Indians greatly need the Water of Life, but they do not want it in European vessels."[30] Accordingly, in conjunction with his *bhakti* Hindu upbringing, Singh's Christian faith journey was one of profound piety and devotion. In his biography of Singh, Appasamy notes that Singh did not approve any idea of God that was not expressed in *bhakti*.[31] Thus, through his intuitive inculturation of the Christian faith, Singh lived out a type of Christian *bhakti*.

Three characteristics mark Singh's Christian *bhakti*.[32] The first is the cultivation of a life of prayer. Akin to the Hindu *bhakti* tradition, prayer, for Singh, is the "greatest theological college in this world."[33] Prayer is not about coming to God with our requests, reciting set formulas, or "speaking in other tongues"; rather, prayer is communion (or union) with God.[34] It is contemplative and meditative. Prayer is the cultivation of a relationship—the "opening of the windows of the soul to let God in."[35] For Singh, prayer demonstrates the highest aspiration or desire for God: "It is breathing and living

---

culture. This can be understood of as a kind of contextual theology. In his Encyclical "Redemptoris Missio," however, Pope John Paul II writes that inculturation is the "intimate transformation of authentic cultural values through their integration in Christianity and the insertion of Christianity in the various human cultures." In this case, the emphasis is more on Christianity's influence on the receptive culture, and less on a mutual intermingling. See John Paul II, "Redemptoris Missio."

29. Boyd, *Indian Christian Theology*, 109.

30. Heiler, *Gospel of Sadhu Sundar Singh*, 232.

31. Appasamy, *Sundar Singh*, 188.

32. These three characteristics are not only drawn from my own reading of Singh's writings but also through a synthesis and extrapolation of how his numerous biographers have understood his theological thought.

33. Appasamy, *Sundar Singh*, 38.

34. Appasamy, *Sundar Singh*, 140.

35. Appasamy, *Sundar Singh*, 238.

God."[36] In other words, prayer for the Christian *bhakta* is beyond language and draws one into a transcendental state, for it is in this state of union that one can be truly receptive to God.

Accordingly, Singh began each day with two hours of prayer, Bible reading, and meditation.[37] It is no surprise then that repetitive mediation on the biblical text comprises the second mark of his Christian *bhakti*. As Appasamy notes, Singh spent a lot of time "devouring" his Urdu New Testament. His method of reading was simple: he would read the same passage over and over again in an attempt to understand the text's meaning.[38] Singh also spent a lot of time meditating on the parables. As his friends often noted, he argued in pictures and drew analogies to demonstrate whichever point he was attempting to make. Very similar to the "Indian Seers and poets" before him,[39] who retained the Indian pattern of inference and analogy, Singh "proved" his points through parabolic analogy, not logical argument.[40] "The Sadhu's mind," Streeter and Appasamy note, "is an overflowing reservoir of anecdote, illustration, epigram, and parable, but he never makes the slightest effort to avoid repetition [of these illustrations]; in fact, he appears to delight in it."[41]

The final mark of Singh's Christian *bhakti* is faith-filled experience. Singh was uninterested in the merely intellectual pursuit of Christianity. Instead, following the *bhakti* tradition, "service" and "reverence" was of utmost importance to him[42]; correct doctrine was less important than how one's life was lived.[43] More specifically, Singh's Christian *bhakti* was so defined by his contemplative

---

36. Moore, *Essential Writings*, 28.

37. Moore, *Essential Writings*, 28.

38. Appasamy, *Sundar Singh*, 159–61.

39. Streeter and Appasamy, *Message of Sadhu Sundar Singh*, 228.

40. Appasamy, *Sundar Singh*, 188. In some schools of Indian thought, analogy (*upamana*) constitutes a separate and legitimate basis of knowledge. See Boyd, *Indian Christian Theology*, 97.

41. Streeter and Appasamy, *Message of Sadhu Sundar Singh*, x.

42. Appasamy, *Sundar Singh*, 30.

43. Appasamy, *Sundar Singh*, 237–38.

experience that it trumped ecclesial, doctrinal, or even scriptural authority.[44] "The first thing in religion," Singh wrote, "is not ritual or works (*karma*), nor a new philosophy (*jnana*), but a new heart, and only those who know and love the crucified and risen Christ can understand fully what this means."[45]

Singh grew up cultivating these disciplines in a Hindu context.[46] Consequently, even after he became a Christian, he was not interested in overcoming Hinduism. Rather, he attempted to relate his newfound faith to the nobler elements of the Hindu religion.[47] It was not that he brought every characteristic of Indian philosophy and religion into his newfound Christianity, but he modified Hindu philosophy in light of his Christian experience.[48] For Singh, Hinduism dug the channels, but Christ, the water, flowed through them.[49] Hinduism had already received insight from the Holy Spirit; Christ simply fulfilled the initial revelation.

Singh's Christian *Bhakti* as a Scriptural Hermeneutic

Without question, Singh's Christian *bhakti* played a tremendous role in how he read the Bible. First, Singh believed that we must read the Bible in faith. Just as he loved the sacred Hindu texts, Singh loved the Bible. For him, it was sweet like sugar.[50] He was convinced of the "wonderful power of the Bible," which he believed should be read in child-like faith. "The language of the word of God" he wrote, "is spiritual; only he who is born of the Spirit can rightly and completely understand it, whether he is a scholar or a

---

44. Heiler, *Gospel of Sadhu Sundar Singh*, 82; and Francis, *Sadhu Sundar Singh*, 94.

45. Boyd, *Indian Christian Theology*, 108.

46. Francis, *Lover of the Cross*, 92.

47. Streeter and Appasamy, *Message of Sadhu Sundar Singh*, 231–33.

48. Appasamy, *Sundar Singh*, 138.

49. Streeter and Appasamy, *Message of Sadhu Sundar Singh*, 232.

50. Streeter and Appasamy, *Message of Sadhu Sundar Singh*, 196.

child."[51] In other words, for Singh, deep calls to deep.[52] There is no secret key required to crack the Bible's code in order to understand it, as long as one reads in faith.

Second, Singh believed that it was necessary for the reader to be in deep communion with God in order to understand the Scripture's meaning. This relationship is cultivated through prayer. For Singh, the Bible is a "mystically inspired creation."[53] Everyday language cannot really express spiritual things in an exhaustive manner. That is why it is so difficult for us to penetrate through the words to the spiritual truth. "To those, however, who are in touch with the author, that is, with the Holy Spirit, all is clear."[54]

Singh clearly believed that the Scriptures were inspired—not in terms of the words themselves, but their "inward meaning."[55] In reading the Bible, Singh's aim was always to understand who God is and, subsequently, who we are in relation to God. Thus, the Bible is not merely "words on a page" that need to be historically dissected in order to confirm (or revoke) its veracity; rather, the text is spiritual and should be read for its outlook on ultimate meaning and reality. In other words, the Bible tells *God's story*. If one is to understand what a biblical text means, one needs to be spiritual and approach the Bible as such. Consequently, as Singh indicated, if one is in constant communion with Christ through prayer, the meaning of the words is made plain.[56]

Third, Singh believed that the reader must surrender completely to God and to the authority of God's Word in order for the meaning to be clear. This was not about believing in the infallibility of the Bible. But through prayerful and faith-filled reading, this type of surrender is possible. For Singh, because Christians who hail from the North Atlantic have lost the "art of prayer," they have

---

51. Heiler, *Gospel of Sadhu Sundar Singh*, 83–84.

52. See Psalm 42:7.

53. Heiler, *Gospel of Sadhu Sundar Singh*, 83.

54. Heiler, *Gospel of Sadhu Sundar Singh*, 84.

55. Streeter and Appasamy, *Message of Sadhu Sundar Singh*, 201.

56. Streeter and Appasamy, *Message of Sadhu Sundar Singh*, 202. See also Boyd, *Indian Christian Theology*, 95.

also lost hold of the central truth of the deity of Christ.[57] Consequently, European and North American Christians from the USA and Canada are no longer able to read in faith and, therefore, cannot understand what the biblical text means. Singh felt that the Bible has the power to show us our faults and shortcomings, but due to "higher methods," we set out to find fault with it. We are always looking for mistakes. "It is no wonder," he wrote, "that people can't understand what the text is saying!"[58] By reading in this way, Singh saw European and North American Christians as suffering from a spiritual "influenza" for which we need to be inoculated.

Singh's three ways of reading Scripture—faith-filled reading, prayerful reading, and surrendered reading—was his method of inoculation. Christian *bhakti*, such as Singh's, underscores a legitimate hermeneutic by which Indians cultivate the art of reading and, consequently, understand the Scriptures. Singh's approach, I believe, is how many Indian people continue to read the Bible in Canada.

Christian *Bhakti*, Knowing God, and Reading Scripture Faithfully in Canada

To conclude, I want to espouse two things based on what I have just said about Sadhu Sundar Singh's Christian *bhakti* and how Indian Christians read the Bible in Canada. First, this method is, in many ways, out of step with the approach of most mainline Euro Canadian churches. Without genuine faith in the salvific work of Christ, however, Christian *bhakti* as an Indian method of hermeneutics is futile. Singh remarked that while he did not desire to condemn theologians and biblical critics outright, he thought that the tendency in European and North American thinking to "doubt and deny everything" was very unfortunate. For him, theologians and biblical critics trained in European epistemologies had completely lost all sense of spiritual reality. He maintained, "You must stop

---

57. Heiler, *Gospel of Sadhu Sundar Singh*, 105.

58. Heiler, *Gospel of Sadhu Sundar Singh*, 108.

examining spiritual truths like dry bones! You must break open the bones and take in the life-giving marrow!"[59]

In my lived experience with Indian Christians in Canada, questions of historical veracity as it applies to reading the Bible are valuable and interesting, but penultimate. Instead, comprehending the meaning of the biblical text and the personal transformation that takes place through faithfully meditating upon the biblical text is crucial. The Bible is to be read, talked about, believed, and observed, even when what it says is confusing, troubling, or infuriating. Bible reading is an exercise in struggle—a struggle that, with perseverance, eventually delivers blessing. This approach to reading the Bible is not about certainty in historical facts that confirm the accuracy of the biblical text, but the blessing of knowing God in fullness, namely, union with God.

Second, this approach is difficult to live out in the North Atlantic context because it necessitates surrendering to an authority beyond us. Concerning Europe and North America, Singh made a challenging comment. He wrote, "It is not enough to know *about* Jesus Christ, you must *know* Him."[60] Our Eurocentric Enlightenment assumptions—e.g., autonomy, individualism, and rationalism—often allow us to think that we control what is to be known. Therefore, it is felt that knowing "about Christ" suffices. The aim of Christian *bhakti*, however, is to know God. Indo-Canadian Christians read the Bible in this unique way for a particular purpose. Though it is similar in many ways, this goes beyond a simple evangelical reading. For Indian Christians, I contend, the art of reading Scripture lies not in taking a "step back" from the text or being "objective" about what is read, but that through reading (i.e., entering the biblical story), we encounter God and thereby find ourselves. Thus, the Indian Christian, like Singh, reads the biblical text and, consequently, understands. By focusing on simply knowing "about" God, Christians steeped in the ways of European culture, values, and traditions have lost the ability to cultivate a relationship with God. Following Singh, they have become like a

59. Moore, *Essential Writings*, 101.

60. Francis, *Lover of the Cross*, 503. Emphasis added.

stone that water has been unable to penetrate—beautiful on the outside, dry on the inside.[61] The objective of Christian *bhakti*, however, is to be radiant inside and out.

I have argued here that Christian *bhakti*, as exemplified by the life and thought of Sadhu Sundar Singh, is an Indian hermeneutic that is observed by many Indian Christians living in Canada. The challenge remains as to whether Canadians of European descent who also desire to read and understand the Scripture will take up the challenge of reading in this prayerful, faith-filled, and surrendered way. This is not a simple path. Reading in this way requires a conversion of cultures or, at least, an acceptance of an alternate cosmology. For the Hindu *bhakta* and the Christian *bhakta*, union with God is the purpose of human existence. Thus, at the very least, the reader of European descent living in Canada must challenge whatever assumptions they hold about what "union with God" may mean and take on a primarily Indian understanding. Following Singh, such union is spiritual, contemplative, devout, transcendental, universal, mystical, and blissful (*ananda*). Christian *bhakti* is also Christocentric. In Hindu cosmology, Gnosticism is not willful heresy; it is simply a way of understanding the world, reading the Bible, and encountering the Christ in an alternate—though still legitimate—way. Consequently, if one looks eastward and desires to know God and be one with God, then Christian *bhakti* is potentially a scriptural hermeneutic that can be embraced by all.

---

61. Moore, *Essential Writings*, 98.

7

First Peoples, Narrative, and Bible Translation

RAY ALDRED AND
CATHERINE ALDRED-SHULL[1]

Introduction

LIKE ANYONE ELSE, I bring to the Bible a set of preconceived notions and understandings. Over the years, however, these preconceptions have changed. In the beginning of my theological career, I thought my job was to read the Bible and find within it little nuggets of truth, biblical principles, and propositions; I thought I was supposed to find a set of truth statements. That was the good stuff; the stuff that would make me a proficient theologian and would keep me secure in my faith. To the contrary, about halfway through my Master of Divinity degree, I found that my faith had become a dry set of intellectual assents unconnected to the passion I had felt in my early experiences with the Bible. My biblical principles had become more important than the gospel story itself, and this left me with a faith that was dry and emotionless. A friend of mine once said that, "Those Pentecostal preachers have one thing right,

1. Catherine Aldred-Shull aided in the research of this essay as well as editing and rewriting the second draft.

without feeling or emotion, people won't do anything."[2] With this in mind, I began to wonder what it would be like to read the Bible like a *Nēhiyaw*—a Cree person. More specifically, I wondered what would happen if I began to consider the Bible as *ācimowin* (meaning "story" or, more literally, "telling a story") rather than as a collection of propositional truths.

I began both to read and to listen to the *story* of Scripture. I did not want to *read* it as if I had control over it, I wanted to *hear* it as story. My identity as a *Nēhiyaw* allowed me to access and utilize the memories and understandings of my people, a people with a keen understanding of how stories work. Through this process, I began to experience the Bible story not only with my head but also with my heart. The gospel story took me in and I was transported to a place where I recognized humor I hadn't recognized before. I heard and saw things with the eyes of my heart, and this brought me back to a good place. I was beginning to uncover a truth that was much too big to be contained in mere theological presuppositions. This truth was something that could only be received in the depths of my being; and so, the truth of the Bible took me in and was translated into my heart language.

As it turns out, the Bible story is a big enough story that it could take in a First Nations boy. It was and is in my heart; it has become part of my flesh and has taken in my flesh. This is the job of translation: to put the gospel story, the canon of Scripture, into the heart language of all people. The hope in this process is that the gospel story might be taken in and, in turn, it takes in new peoples and new generations of people, so that they might be changed into who the Creator made them to be. In other words, Bible translation ultimately aims at enfleshing the Word in human hearts that are part of the community of God. Because people are in a constant state of change, the job of translation and interpretation is never done.[3]

2. Personal conversation with Adrian Jacobs at a meeting of Aboriginal Task Force of the Evangelical Fellowship of Canada, 2001.

3. This article operates with the understanding that the title "Interpreter" can be justifiably used interchangeably with "Translator." This claim is

Translation is not something for which one can buy an app, although this is not to say that computer software is not of great assistance in the process. Translation, particularly of the gospel story, is something that requires flesh and blood. It is not simply a matter of trying to pass some universal meaning from one set of linguistic symbols and encode it into another. The Bible comes to us in the form of a story that attempts to capture the acts of the triune God in the language of humans. Scripture is taken into a community that welcomes it, interprets what the gospel story means for them, and, in turn, this community is shaped by the message in this book—by this gospel story.

In translation, we are not simply shifting letters and words around, choosing their equivalent in another language in an attempt to communicate. Paul Ricoeur speaks to the complicated nature of translation. He describes translation as a reflection of the translator entering into dialogue with a text to express its meaning.[4] This dialogue between translator and text is what opens the text up to what he calls a *surplus of meaning*.[5]

Each of us has a set of culturally-conditioned, preconceived understandings that shape the way we read or listen to the Bible's message. Each of us changes the Bible in our encounter with it, even if we are not professional translators or theologians, because our understanding stresses only certain parts of the story. In the same way, our encounter with the Bible changes us as we appropriate the knowledge it contains.

When I read or listen to the biblical story, I try to employ a hermeneutic of love which guides my interaction with it. By hermeneutic of love, I mean a dynamic of mutuality that takes place between a people and the biblical story: as a people encounter the gospel, its message changes because of the ethno-cultural identity

---

supported in the and philosophy of Paul Ricoeur, who uses the titles of "Interpreter" and "Translator" interchangeably in his work on translation and Biblical hermeneutics. See also Pol, *Task of the Interpreter*; and Green and Turner, *Between Two Horizons*.

4. Ricoeur, *Interpretation Theory*, 12.

5. Ricoeur, *Interpretation Theory*, 31.

and history of those people—but those people also change as a result of encountering the gospel. Neither the scripture nor the people become something they were not meant to be.

This hermeneutic of love, however, has not always characterized interactions between the First Nations of Canada and the Western European colonizers, specifically in the latter's translations of the Bible into First Nations languages. In spite of this, the gospel continues to be appropriated by Indigenous people, who both take in the gospel and are taken in by it. Nevertheless, this process could be enriched by the kind of Bible translation and interpretation that values and takes the communal, narratival identity of Canada's Indigenous peoples seriously.

In this piece, I intend to argue that through the work of translation into indigenous languages, the gospel is both taken in by the receptor culture[6] and takes in this said culture in return. I will propose that this task requires a hermeneutic of love on a trajectory toward a new community that recognizes the inherent value of diversity.

The Need for a Different Kind of Translation

The indigenous peoples of Canada continue to carry out the task of self-defining their theology, and Bible translation is an important part of that. Indigenous peoples bring an important perspective to the work of Bible translation and interpretation because our identities and spiritualties are defined by our understanding of how stories work. For example, take the narrative memory of the historical formation of treaties, which is essential to Cree peoples' present identity. The claims that the Cree Nation makes on the basis of these narratives not only necessitate an assertion of historicity and reliability but also embrace the dynamic/stable qualities of these histories:

> The dynamic nature of Cree narrative memory . . . could be conceived of as an organism, growing and shifting.

6. By receptor culture, I mean the group who receives the translation.

Nonetheless, like all organisms, Cree narrative memory has a structure within the parameters of possibility, and there is a great deal of stability . . . Humility is a primary characteristic of Cree Narrative memory and acknowledges that narratives are open-ended. There is no end to how they can be interpreted[7]

Among many of the indigenous nations of the Americas, there are stories and legends about people having visions of a race of people who would come and bring something good, sometimes even bringing a black book. My friend Adrian Jacobs tells the story of the Hopi, whom he had an opportunity to visit a few years back. They tell the story of Pahana, their long-lost, white brother, who would come one day and, together with them, complete what was lacking in both groups' (the indigenous and the white) understanding. The legend with which I am most familiar is among the Plains Cree. They say that Jesus himself met with them in a place just outside of Regina, just prior to his ascension. He told them that the white man was coming and that the plains people were to learn from them what was the best. The best they had was the Bible and, of course, Jesus. It is because of these multiple stories among the First Nations and the fact that their stories connect with the Bible story that it is essential that a narrative approach to the gospel includes translation into indigenous languages. Such translations will have to go beyond linguistic and technical matters and include the cultural and socio-historical understanding of indigenous peoples.

Regardless of the historicity of these legends about the Bible, their existence is evidence that the Bible and the gospel story have become a part of the sacred Narrative of indigenous peoples of the Americas. It is not enough, however, that the Bible is considered sacred—whether as a book upon a shelf or part of a legend. Stories are alive. The Bible must be heard! It must be interpreted! It must be lived!

---

7. McLeod, *Cree Narrative Memory*, 42.

Our Past: Colonial Modernity
(Civilization and the Bible)

The history of Bible translation in Canada is a complicated one. It is the popular opinion that until quite recently, most First Nations languages have functioned in a primarily oral context. The introduction of syllabic writing came only in the mid-1800s.[8] This shift from orality to literacy is directly linked to the first Bible translations into First Nations languages, as part of the larger evangelistic goals of the first Christian missionaries.

When the Western European explorers arrived on the Northern coastline of the Americas, their intention was to extend the boundaries of their own colonial empires. They also sought to extend their own theological empire by converting the "savages" they encountered in these new lands. Whether wild lands or wild people, the goal was to "cultivate" and "civilize" both. They found justification to do this by *allegorizing* the message of the Bible, which provided support for colonial expansion and for mythologizing the identity of indigenous peoples.

The idea of "Manifest Destiny," as believed by many Western Europeans, was used by colonial powers to justify the taking of more and more territories in Canada. The idea of the "wild other" was also used to legitimate their attack on indigenous peoples. Every effort was made to use this propaganda to assuage the conscience of the early settlers and to convince indigenous people that their own identities were an obstacle for "development." Not only did the colonial powers see indigenous people as savages but the indigenous people themselves began to hate their own identity as well.

The process of civilization also meant elimination of the wilderness and the people of that wilderness. Reverend John West, the first CMS (Christian Missionary Society) missionary in British North America, wrote in his journal of the efforts to export British culture to indigenous people. According to West, the land of the Natives (the wilderness) was not desirable. He and his fellow

---

8. Demers et al., *Beginning of Print Culture*, xi.

missionaries saw themselves as cultivating the land in spiritual ways that would also lead to cultivation of the actual, physical land: "To cultivate the heath is to convert the heathen, and vice versa."[9]

The intent of missionary work was to replace the cultures, traditions, and languages of the First Peoples and give them a different story, a different history, and a different understanding of God and theology. This meant that the first translation work was not overly concerned with putting the Bible into the language of the people but rather with communicating the theology of those doing the work of translation. The goal was to *civilize* the people with the gospel story. In a sense, the Bible became part and parcel of a kind of colonial myth or allegory. Under such an allegorical reading, the Bible was understood as propagating a particular Western, European conception of the kingdom of God to which the First Nations were required to convert. In this way, colonial European powers interpreted their own progress as the eschatological culmination of the kingdom—the gospel was a metaphor of their own progress. This produced a translation method in which "cultural replacement" was the desired outcome of Bible translation.

Take, for example, the work of Protestant translator John Horden, the first Bishop of Moosonee. Horden saw his translation work as a way to confront the Oblates, to "counteract their fatal influences and fortify the midst of the people against insidious attacks."[10] He feared that a Roman Catholic translation and interpretation of the Bible would result in more converts to Roman Catholicism. It might even be suggested that Horden held the belief that it was his role (and the role of the Christian authorities that would succeed him) to guide his "Indian flock" into proper belief and Christian understanding. His perspective is evident in a pastoral letter he wrote in 1882, after a three-year absence from the Moosenee area. In it, he spoke with the authority and style akin to letters of the Apostle Paul: "I should be glad if I were able to send you other ministers to teach you things: just now you have had two; don't cease to pray for them, to hear them, and to help them.

9. Austin and Scott, *Canadian Missionaries, Indigenous Peoples*, 22.
10. Long, "John Horden," 86–97.

But when God's minister is unable to go to you, these little books will reach you and will dwell with you."[11]

In the colonial societies of Canada and the United States of America, conversion became synonymous with becoming civilized or white.[12] In a discussion I witnessed among indigenous Anglicans in Canada, it was pointed out that even the word "Anglican," a marker for denomination or Christian identity, translates into Cree as "white." One Cree speaker pointed out that a pamphlet printed in syllabics with the title of Anglican Indigenous Theological Education, when translated into Cree, reads, "White Indigenous Theological Education." These contradictions, which began during the colonial empire, can still be observed today.[13]

John Friesen writes, "Despite efforts to update source materials, most libraries in North America are still well-stocked with books depicting Native people in uncomplimentary and inflammatory ways."[14] Not only did academic writing characterize indigenous people as "noble savages" but also regarded them as almost unconscious inhabitants who just happened to arrive in the empty lands of the region thousands of years before the Europeans. It is in this way that Western European colonization was justified; the First Nations were viewed as inferior, prior immigrants who had no claim to the land.[15] The myth that indigenous people need to be civilized or fixed continues. This myth feeds "rhetoric of progress" and remains tied to a particular form of Christianity that continues to make its power felt.

Another example of this can be found in a *Dictionary of the Cree Language* published in 1865:

> When efforts were first made to translate the Bible, some long and cumbersome words were introduced to answer the scripture terms, as, for instance *kichikiesi-*

11. Horden, "Cree Pastoral," vii.

12. Charleston, "Reflections on a Revival," 73.

13. See Truth and Reconciliation Commission, *Honoring the Truth, Reconciling for the Future.*

14. Friesen, *Aboriginal Spirituality*, 27–28.

15. Friesen, *Aboriginal Spirituality*, 31.

kooweutooskayakun, angel, i.e. a heavenly servant, but
now these clumsy compounds are, for the most part,
abandoned and the English word are substituted. The
Christian Indians who are under regular ministerial
instruction soon learn to connect the proper ideas with
such expressions.[16]

Concrete examples of these "anglo-cized" terms can be found in the
aforementioned Moose Cree Translation, by Horden, above. The
word "angels" is rendered *ēncala* in syllabic Cree, which is a transliteration from the English word. Similarly, the word "messenger" is
rendered using the transliteration *nimisyawēk* in Reverend William
Mason's translation of the Bible into Plains Cree.

In these and other ways, the first Canadian Bible translations
aided the slow and deliberate eradication of indigenous languages.
Such work did not necessarily prioritize the transmission of the
gospel story into the language system of the people; rather, it was
inordinately preoccupied with translating the "white" theological
underpinnings of Western Europeans. The focus was not on giving First Nations people the gospel story but on bringing them
into submission to a foreign institution and culture. As Mi'kmaq
scholar Terry LeBlanc observes:

> Mission to Native peoples necessitated that Native
> peoples do three things: (1) Adopt European ideas of
> material value and wealth connected to resources of the
> land; (2) Accept the growing social-liberal way of life
> with autonomous personal well-being and individual
> competitiveness; and (3) Sever connection to belief that
> the totality of creation is possessed of a spiritual nature.[17]

Our Present (Orality and Literacy in Tension)

The task of First Nations Bible translation today is further complicated as indigenous peoples *themselves* attempt to communicate

16. Watkins, *Dictionary of the Cree Language*, xx.
17. LeBlanc, "Residential School: Policy, Power and Mission."

the central core of their traditions and cultures while remaining faithful to the biblical text. One could think of these contemporary translation attempts as a historical-grammatical quest for the core of indigenous cultures. The problem today is that Western European and Euro-North American cultures and intellectual traditions continue to determine what exactly "grammatical" and "literal" mean. One could suggest that using the present standards of translation yield a result where translation continues to have a Western European and Euro-North American accent.

It is becoming increasingly common for Bible societies to train indigenous people to do the work of translation. However, Western European versions of theology play a dominant role even in these projects, despite the fact that the theologies of Western Europeans are no longer always overtly attempting to replace indigenous theologies. Western European and Euro-North American culture continues to exercise its influence upon the scriptures. In many ways, the Bible is a construct of the North Atlantic mindset, not particularly at home in many indigenous languages which remain primarily oral and performative in nature. For example, some indigenous people use a Cree translation from the nineteenth century written in syllabics. The vast majority of Cree readers, however, cannot read syllabics because the preferred method of writing Cree today is in roman orthography. Then again, there are fluent Cree speakers who cannot read Cree at all, given that Cree is still used primarily in an oral context.

In the same way, the translations of the Bible into Cree do not draw from the original source languages (Greek and Hebrew) but use English versions instead.[18] The adaptation of an English text to an indigenous language may be preferred to replacement of indigenous languages altogether, but it proves to be of limited value to the development of Christian indigenous communities on par with Western European and Euro-North American expressions. The resulting translations do not seek to find ways to express the gospel in the heart languages of indigenous peoples. Rather, the outcome is a Western European and Euro-North

18. Most notably the Good News Translation or the King James translation.

American false representation of what an indigenous conception of the gospel would look like. In the end, all the effort and time spent producing these translations are often for naught because nobody uses them.[19]

James Maxey makes this point in his book *Orality to Orality*, noting that many Christians in Euro-North America and Western Europe understand the Bible as a literary production, like many other books produced today. They understand that access to the Bible is uniquely available by literacy, a type of individual, silent deciphering of written code: "The transmission of the Bible into other parts of the world . . . has been accompanied by the literary agenda."[20] In other words, since the Bible is translated by Western Europeans, the rules of Western European literature govern how the story is told, even though these rules are distinctly foreign to indigenous languages that have a primarily oral history, including the biblical text. This begs the question: if a language contains an inherent bent toward orality, why wouldn't you translate it in a way that would enhance the ability for the story to be told or performed in the community?

We have already suggested that indigenous understandings of story and oral narrative memory allow for a text or story to have both dynamic and stable qualities simultaneously. It could also be suggested that the biblical storytellers (such as the writer of the Gospel of John) might have shared this understanding of the dynamic quality of memory: "For John, the memory of Jesus is a fluid, dynamic, and charismatic entity that can readily adapt itself to new situations."[21] The presence of four forms of the gospel narrative in the New Testament, each presenting the story in a distinct way, further expresses a sense of the diversity of the gospel tradition, which might also demonstrate a level of freedom felt by each of the authors; that is, to adapt the narrative to suit their audience or situation.

19. See Cox, *Impact of Christian Missions*.
20. Maxey, *Orality to Orality*, 1.
21. Thatcher, "Why John Wrote a Gospel," 81.

However, significant changes occurred with the development of a standardized "canon" of biblical texts and the establishment of print literacy. Both of these changes resulted in what Walter Ong describes as a "fixed point of few."[22] The canonization process was a way of preserving specific textual traditions. It also marked a shift from the priority of ritual repetition of texts to doing interpretive work on texts.[23] The interpretive activity moved from focusing on the stability of essential story, which is the goal of oral tradition, to stability of text, which is the exact word of the story.[24] The process of canonization resulted in the cessation of the "living stream of tradition."[25] Let me suggest, however, that it is through translation and interpretation of these words that the stories of the Bible are kept alive.

Our Future (Contextualization, the Hermeneutic of Love, and Heart Language Translation)

There is a need for the kind of translation that is truly dynamic and encompasses the gospel story and the stories of peoples encountering the gospel. It is a translation in which a given culture takes the gospel story in and is taken in by the gospel, resulting in a translation that truly conforms to the hermeneutics of love. This hermeneutic allows people to be who God created them to be. Consequently, translation requires individuals to question the theories and beliefs that have guided Bible translations thus far. It also requires that the people doing the translation be indigenous people themselves—scholars who are familiar with or have access to both biblical languages and the languages of their respective communities. Only in this way will the resulting translation be faithful to the Bible story and speak in the heart language of that people.

22. Ong, *Orality and Literacy*, 132.
23. Assmann, *Religion and Cultural Memory*, 121.
24. Davis, *Oral Biblical Criticism*, 14.
25. Assman, *Religion and Cultural Memory*, 120.

This kind of translation and hermeneutic of love aims to contextualize the canon of Scripture within the cultural context of the people. When describing contextualization, Leslie Newbigin said that the gospel must be put into categories of the receptor culture.[26] If we allow that contextualization is necessary in any translation or interpretive work,[27] it follows that translations into indigenous languages must pay attention to communal and narratival characteristics of indigenous identities. These characteristics are imbued with an understanding of story that brings immense value to the stories in the Bible.

While teaching a course at the Vancouver School of Theology called "The Resurrection of Story," I conducted an experiment. I read a passage of scripture to a group of First Nations people from Luke 10. The story tells of an instance when Jesus sends out seventy disciples. When they come back, they tell Jesus about casting out demons and healing people, and Jesus responds by saying, "I saw Satan falling from heaven." My experiment had to do with that last phrase: Satan falling from heaven. I asked my students, "to what does that phrase refer?" Now anyone growing up in a Western European evangelical tradition will offer suggestions that this refers to the fall of Lucifer at some point in the past. But the story is actually referring to the acts of the seventy, as they went out and cast out demons. In a sense, Satan is being cast down; that is how the story works. I wanted to know if these indigenous people, with little academic education, would understand this point. They did! I suggest that they were able to understand because they know how story works.

It is for this reason that I am proposing that the task of translation work must fit the categories of First Nations. Their understanding and stories are performative, and this characteristic must be preserved. Translation must take the way that story works in indigenous cultures and their categories seriously. In terms of categories, for example, indigenous peoples place a greater emphasis upon location than upon time. Western European and Euro-North

26. Newbigin, *Foolishness to the Greek*.

27. See Ricoeur, *Interpretation Theory*.

Americans are enamored with time. It is not that one is right and the other is wrong but that they are different perspectives—and that makes a difference in how things are translated. George Tinker, a Native American scholar, points out that the locative emphasis of indigenous people means that certain repetition of the location performs a theological task within the gospel story. He discusses the Mark 10:46 story of the beggar sitting by the way (Greek *odos*). As he shows, the NRSV translates it as roadside, while the NASB translates it as road, the NIV as roadside, and the King James translates it as highway. None of these versions link it with the obvious *inclusio* in Mark 10:52, when the blind man joins Jesus on the *odos*. This word is not translated "way," but, in English, one has to work harder at making the connection of place because the focus is upon time. The literary values of Western European culture dictate that the repetition of *odos* be broken up.[28] In an oral tradition, however, the movement of Jesus is through time as well as place; he has come in the flesh.

The gospel must be put into the heart language of the people. This includes their social aspirations. First Nations people aspire to continue to live as people upon the land that has been our home and mother for all these years. A translation in which those in control are non-indigenous does not speak to the indigenous aspiration to be self-theologizing. Translation organizations will need to raise money to not only translate the Bible *for* indigenous people but to train indigenous people *to do* the work themselves. Indigenous people are not merely assets to be used by Western European and Euro-North American translation consultants; rather, the consultant themselves should be indigenous.

Viewed in this way, contextualization does not only intend to produce someone just like "me" but also seeks to provide a method for translation and interpretation that allows for a surplus of possibilities. The goal must not be to replace or adapt one set of ideas to a new situation but allow for new audiences to expand and extend the vision and identity that God the Creator has been working to produce in them.

28. Tinker, *Spirit and Resistance*, 95–96.

Final Remarks: The Fourth World

The future of Bible translation can never sustain itself based on isolated groups of peoples and cultures who merely tolerate each other. In *The Nature of Doctrine*, George Lindbeck wondered if it were possible that each group began with the gospel story as the first thing, then each group, with their own presuppositions, could make doctrinal decisions that shape their identity; in the end, we all could share that we have a mutual beginning point.[29] I have suggested that this is a worthy goal but must not merely end with people isolated from one another. We must endeavor to produce a body of translations that reflect the diversity of creation, that represent a dialogue between communities, and that seeks a *telos* or goal that will see the value of *the many* and not just the one. It is through this dialogue that we are brought together around the gospel story as our shared narrative.

Claiming the gospel as our shared narrative does not mean that we aim for translations whereby everyone reads, speaks, and thinks in the same way. It does not mean that we seek to eradicate differences between cultural groups. Such a perspective would signal a regression to a colonial mentality that seeks to absorb all things into its own version. The indigenous scholar Sophie Mc-Call notes that Western Europeans and Euro-North Americans are very quick to want to close what they perceive to be cultural gaps between themselves and others. But she suggests that these cultural gaps are the space for fruitful collaboration.[30] Moreover, to say that one group has arrived at the final translation or interpretation would reduce all other translations as inferior and reinforce the Eurocentric-North Atlantic status quo. We need a translation that aims not for an imagined world in the past, a colonial world, or even a post-colonial world; we need the fourth[31] world, where each

29. Lindbeck, *Nature of Doctrine*.

30. See McCall, "What the Map Cuts Up."

31. I am using the term "fourth world" as used by Manuel et al., *Fourth World*. According to George Manuel and Michael Posluns, the "third world" was reacting to Western politics and adapting to Western technology. As they put it, the "fourth world" is about Indigenous North Americans attempting to

of us, with our own voice, join in the choir of voices proclaiming the gospel of the Lord Jesus Christ. As Psalm 40:7–8 reads: "Here I am; in the scroll of the book it is written of me. I delight to do your will, O my God; your law is within my heart."

---

co-exist with the West. It is also about Indigenous reality being deeply connected with the land. Again, this is not primarily about a political statement but rather about a deep spirituality connected to place

8

Visible but Voiceless Minorities no More

New Readings of the Bible in Canada

GOSNELL L. YORKE

Introduction

As a vast, beautiful, sparsely-populated, and yet proud and productive member of the G7, Canada seeks to derive maximum cultural, economic, and socio-political benefits from the rich heritage of its diverse inhabitants. These inhabitants encompass those of African descent, Asian ancestry, European extraction, Indigenous Peoples (including First Nations, Métis, and Inuit), and those of Latin American origin.

Consistent with this overarching national objective—albeit after some protracted political and sometimes rancorous debates—in 1971, Canada committed itself to an official policy of "Multiculturalism within a Bilingual Framework." This was a nation-building attempt to bridge the obvious divide between its two dominant Euro-communities (anglophone and francophone) and its minoritized communities, including the First Peoples, who are usually lumped together as the so-called "Visible Minorities," pointing to all those who are of non-European descent.

Such an ostensibly commendable policy was not driven simply by Canada's concerted attempt to embrace all of its diverse inhabitants creatively, constructively, and comprehensively nor was it merely motivated by the country's ardent desire to further advance its development agenda. Rather, such a policy was meant to project to the international community a nation that is tolerant of diversity, inclusive of others, and one in which the rights of all are protected and promoted.

Embedded within such a policy, however, was the seemingly irresolvable tension between the acknowledgment of the multicultural make-up of the country and giving pride of place to the two dominant Euro-communities in Canada. That is, both English and French were foregrounded as the two sole official languages. With language being such an integral part of culture, it is not entirely surprising that minoritized Canadians, whose language did not enjoy the privileged position of official status (but were left to be best employed and enjoyed privately), invariably have not felt and continue to not feel part of the Canadian mainstream.[1] Feelings of what might appear to be racism-induced rejection and marginalization were and still are, to varying degrees, the order of the day for many—if not most—of Canada's minoritized communities. Further, this overt bilingual bias (English and French) finds reflection in the country's highly developed bi-legal judicial system, encompassing both English Common Law and its French Civil counterpart.

Language is an integral part of culture, but so is religion. Canada, in spite of its multi-religious make-up and what some might now see as its hearty embrace of a post-Enlightenment-inspired drift towards secularism (as well as its attendant successors, modernity and postmodernism), is still very much informed and influenced by its Judeo-Christian roots and values. These are values which are mainly embedded within and emanate from its dominant and still dominating English and French foundations—including its instituting documents, such as the *British North America Act* (1867), which established Canada as a nation. This Euro-centric

1. Haque, *Multiculturalism.*

religious state of affairs is perhaps best captured in the somewhat contentious Preamble to the 1982 Canadian Charter of Rights and Freedoms in which Canada, as a country, explicitly submits itself to "the supremacy of God and the rule of law."

Major-General Georges Philias Vanier (1888–1967), the distinguished Canadian soldier, diplomat, and the first francophone Governor General of Canada, not only addresses the on-going anglophone/francophone-induced tension which still poses some socio-political and economic challenges to attempts at nation-building but also echoes the underlying theological conviction to which we have just referred. He writes as follows: "Canada owes it to the world to remain united, for no other lesson is more badly needed than the one our unity can supply: the lesson that diversity need not be the cause for conflict, but, on the contrary, may lead to richer and nobler living. I pray to God that we go forward hand in hand."[2]

In light of this reality, it is most fitting that some attempt be made, finally, to reflect on what the Bible, as the *Grundnorm* or foundational theological document of the Church, ought to mean to those within the Canadian Christian community who are numbered among the country's not-inconsiderable number of minoritized Canadians. Present "guesstimates," for example, suggest that minoritized Canadians constitute as much as one third of the country's population of some thirty-six million.

In light of the above, the time is past due for a voice to be given to the hitherto "voiceless visibles." This is a clarion call which is entirely congruent with the contemporary goings-on in academia, not the least of which would include Bible translation and, more broadly, biblical studies. Also, it is a call which has been emanating with ever increasing intensity and impatience not only from the "Global South" of Africa, Latin America, the Caribbean, and elsewhere in the world[3] but also from among those who inhabit what might

2. Government of Canada, "Georges Philias Vanier."

3. See Dube and Wafula, eds. *Postcoloniality*; Yorke, "Foreword," (2013) ix–xi; Yorke, "Foreword," (2014) xiii–xiv; Moore and Segovia, *Postcolonial Biblical Criticism*; and Moore and Segovia, "AfriCanadian Theology," 1–12.

best be described as pockets of the "Global South" in the "Global North"—to which Canada rightly purports to belong.

Essentially, this is what this groundbreaking volume is really all about. As one of its interlocutors, I wish to highlight some of the salient issues to which the six contributors to this volume have addressed themselves. Foundational to this theological and hermeneutical enterprise is the settled and now widely shared consciousness and conviction that one's perspective, one's place, one's space, or one's location inevitably plays an important role (consciously or not) in one's attempt to make the Bible contextually relevant and meaningful to its readers.[4]

It is this conviction which has influenced all the contributors of this volume. It is a conviction that runs like Ariadne's thread throughout the volume as a whole. Summed up in the expression "narratival hermeneutics," all the contributors, to varying degrees, seek to ground their take on the Bible not only within the context of their own personal stories but, more generally, within the history and traditions of their own ethno-cultural communities as well. This defensible methodological move stems from the recognition that when it comes to the proper interpretation, appropriation, and application of the Bible, there is a dialectical or dialogical interaction between individuality and community; between the personal and the communal.

Such a hermeneutical recognition would seem to run counter to, for some, the still stiflingly predominant Eurocentric paradigm. This is a hegemonic and normative paradigm in which it is sometimes assumed that the proper interpretation of the Bible can best be achieved through the consistent use of the so-called historical-critical method, ably applied by the disengaged individual biblical scholar working independently of others except, perhaps, in scholarly conversation with the similarly-minded— be they dead or alive.[5]

---

4. See Boer and Segovia, *Future of the Biblical Past*; Bailey et al., *They Were All Together*; and Blount et al., *True to Our Native Land*.

5. Cuellar makes the point that "operating in the interstices between contemporary readers and the Bible is a plurality of hermeneutical regimes." See

If anything, Albert Schweitzer, among others, succeeded in shattering this myth of a disengaged "rugged individualism" in his classic *The Quest for the Historical Jesus*. He demonstrated, quite compellingly, without actually making it explicit that, inevitably, the biblical scholar is as immersed in her/his culture and society as the fish is in the sea. That is, in plotting the various Christologies (or is it "Jesusologies"?) which were articulated by the various European scholars of the eighteenth and nineteenth centuries—those whose names he chose to invoke, like Hermann Reimarus, Ernest Renan, David Strauss, and William Wrede—Schweitzer concluded that the Christology of the scholar in question was invariably a reflection of a Jesus made in the scholar's own image, chiefly French bourgeoisie or German upper-class elites. Further, it was an image which sometimes resonated with and was a clear reflection of the larger, national preoccupations and prevailing presuppositions of the time. In other words, there wasn't the neat bifurcation or dichotomy between scholar and society, between the private and the public, as was tacitly assumed.

In this regard, Willi Braun, mentioning both Albert Schweitzer and Rudolf Bultmann, among others, captures the pith and substance of this basic contention exceptionally well. In discussing the scholar's historical construction of the past, he points out that such constructions are not only "deeply embedded in the social, institutional, and disciplinary settings that furnish the historian [biblical scholar] with the motivations and aims but also [embedded in] the conceptual and analytical tools . . . in the first place."[6]

Again, it is in light of this consciousness and conviction that the six contributions in the current volume should be analyzed and appreciated. In my opinion, the six contributors are to be applauded for their unapologetic and explicit embrace of and stubborn commitment to their narratival, hermeneutical approach to the Bible as a way of insisting that, ultimately, the whole hermeneutical enterprise involves a dialectical interaction between themselves as minoritized Canadian Christian theologians and

Cuellar, "Task of Decentering."

6. Braun, "Socio-Rhetorical Interests," 92.

scholars of the biblical text and their own ethno-cultural communities. They emphasize that their ethno-cultural communities do and should play an indispensable role in terms of how the Bible is interpreted, appropriated, and applied.

Engaging the Contributors

With this said, allow me, then, to briefly engage the six contributors whom we can place in two broad categories: (1) HyeRan Kim-Cragg (Korean-Canadian) and Barbara Leung Lai (Chinese-Canadian), both of whom use a specific biblical text upon which to base their reflections; and (2) Ray Alfred (Cree), Alison Hari-Singh (Indo-Canadian), Alan Lun Lai (Chinese-Canadian) and Néstor Medina (Latino/a-Canadian), all of whom write about the hermeneutical implications of engagement with the Bible more generally.

For the most part, I will not merely provide a synopsis of what the contributors have written since, in my view, they have already expressed themselves clearly and compellingly enough. Instead, I wish to cull and quarry from their contributions a few salient points which I consider worth highlighting as one of the interlocutors.

First of all, in looking at the story of Jephthah's daughter as recoded in Judges 11:34–40, in which she weaves both liturgical and feminist considerations into her insightful analysis based on what she refers to as an "inter-positioning approach," HyeRan Kim-Cragg, a pastoral theologian of Korean extraction and someone of relatively modest height, is acutely aware of the "high chair culture" of Canada's two "founding societies" (anglophone and francophone). Such a "high chair culture" makes her sit rather uncomfortably, with her feet dangling in the air instead of being firmly planted on the floor beneath her. Moreover, the high chair does not allow her, as a Korean-Canadian, to sit cross-legged comfortably, as is the custom in her culture. This, for me, is a powerful metaphor of how "out of sync" the dominant Euro-Canadian Christian community (both anglophone and francophone) is with minoritized groups like the Korean-Canadian Christian community.

My only slight dis-ease with Kim-Cragg's otherwise provocative contribution is that she seemed to have limited her interaction with her Canadian ethno-cultural Christian community to those who, like her, were professionally formed as ordained ministers within the Presbyterian Church of Korea. A more inclusive embrace of the community as a whole—encompassing what scholars like Gerald West would refer to as "ordinary readers" in much of his writings—might have been helpful as well.[7]

As for Barbara Leung Lai and Alan Lun Lai, both diasporic Chinese Canadians (*huaquio* [overseas Chinese] à la Alan Lun Lai), the Bible is best appreciated, appropriated, and applied when it is rooted within their rich ethno-cultural Sino-traditions. To illustrate what this might mean in practical hermeneutical terms, Leung Lai, for example, chooses to direct our attention to the obvious skepticism and sense of meaninglessness and anomie which characterizes much of the book of Ecclesiastes, as well as Qoheleth, the Preacher. She then chooses to discuss Ecclesiastes against the backdrop of the Chinese notions of *Xiao Wo* (the "small self") and *Da Wo* (the "bigger whole"). Under the influence of Carol Newsom, Leung Lai also subjects Ecclesiastes to a "cross-the-grains" reading and argues that the book is predominantly an "I-text." Perhaps it should be pointed out here that this "I-stress" or focus on the self is not uniquely Chinese in that it resonates with much of what we encounter in Jamaican Rasta Talk as well.[8]

What I found particularly useful in Alan Lun Lai's contribution is that there is not only a very informative recital of the somewhat checkered, racism-driven history of Chinese people coming to and settling in Canada from various Asian countries (such as Vietnam, Hong Kong, and mainland China itself) but also the explicit grounding of the Bible within Confucian ethics and piety. Given the Confucian stress on constant self-improvement and, perhaps, insufficient attention given to the need for serious involvement in

7. See, for example, West, *Stolen Bible*.
8. See Palmer, *Messianic "I."*

more all-encompassing, socio-political matters, it is not in the least surprising that Chinese Canadians tend to be drawn to the more conservative end of the Christian spectrum in which it is falsely assumed that political engagement and Christian piety should be regarded as polar opposites of each other.[9]

When we turn to Alison Hari-Singh, perhaps driven by the defensible feminist conviction that the personal is political,[10] we are treated to a refreshing foray into identity politics in which much of her discussion about the Bible and how it interfaces with her own diverse Indian culture is autobiographically grounded. In her discussion, she also makes the cardinal point, I think, that Christianity found a much more fertile soil in those places of the sub-continent of India where a strong *bhakti* tradition had already taken root. In addition, she makes the point that Sadhu Sundar Singh (born in 1889) was heavily influential in helping to Indianize Christianity in India.[11] She then argues, by extension, that Singh's Christian *bhakti* provides a heuristic hermeneutic by which many Indian Christians still choose to read the Bible within their transplanted Canadian context and setting.[12]

Where I do part company slightly with Hari Singh, however, is her suggestion that this *bhakti*-induced distinction between knowing and doing—between the cognitive and the affective or between belief and behavior—is unique to the Indian community in its contemporary hermeneutical approach and contextually driven reading of the Bible in Canada. The truth is, we would find this sort of distinction repeatedly made, for example, within

9. See Boesak and Young, *Radical Reconciliation*.

10. See Schüssler Fiorenza, *Democratizing Biblical Studies*; and Smith, ed., *I Found God in Me*.

11. Also instructive here is Roger Hedlund. See Hedlund, "India's New Era," 225–37.

12. Incidentally, some of Singh's views would later be echoed in Mahatma Ghandi's conviction in which he is reported to have lambasted Western or Eurocentric Christians for placing a much greater emphasis on knowing about or having a more intellectual encounter with the risen Christ rather than coming to a personal knowledge of Him and, in so doing, emulating his life of self-sacrifice and service.

earlier Afro-slave societies in North America (including Canada) and in the Caribbean as well.[13]

Néstor Medina, in directing our attention to the newly arrived burgeoning Latina/o Canadian community, presents us with what he refers to as a lived-hermeneutics in which we see a dialectical hermeneutical interaction between personal story and ethno-cultural community. Since Medina self-identifies as a confessing Christian within the vibrant Pentecostal tradition, it is not in the least surprising that he grounds much of his discussion within that orally and pneumatologically driven tradition as well. This then tempts him to extrapolate from that tradition to make claims about the larger Canadian Christian Latina/o community as a whole.

The point worth making here, I think, is that, contrary to the simplistic and stereotypical assumption sometimes made about the Pentecostal community, Canadian Latina/o Christians, according to Medina, do not engage in a strict literalist reading of the Bible. Medina argues that, given the dialectical or dialogical interaction or interchange between the personal and the communal, the one and the many, individuality and community, and the often-uninviting context within which life is being lived in Canada, Bible reading and interpretation cannot help but be rather nuanced. In my view, this important observation is entirely congruent with the global Afro-Christian community as well—encompassing those who are situated or located within the displaced, dispersed, and largely dispossessed African diaspora.[14]

Finally, I now fix and focus my attention on Ray Alfred, a Cree biblical theologian of evangelical extraction. In doing so, I concur wholeheartedly with him that Bible translation is not an innocent activity. This proves to be the case in spite of how well-intentioned the early Euro-Canadian missionary translators may have been. Instead, the translation of the Bible into indigenous receptor languages—such as Moose Cree, Plains Cree, or any other language spoken in the Global South and translated by those from

13. For that, see Erskine, *Plantation Church*; Felder, *Stony the Road We Trod*; Felder, *Troubling Biblical Waters*; and Shreve, *AfriCanadian Church*.

14. See Page, *Reading Israel's Scriptures*; and Yorke, "Blacks and the Bible."

the Global North—has been informed and influenced by all sorts of sometimes unarticulated ideological and cultural assumptions which invariably have counterproductive and dis-empowering consequences for its readers.[15]

Conclusion

In the language of Qoheleth—the Preacher and, perhaps, Epilogist, à la Barbara Leung Lai (see Eccl 12:13)—here, then, is the conclusion of the whole matter: this long-overdue volume comes as a confident and clarion call for us to take cognizance of and to listen to the erstwhile muted hermeneutical voice of all minoritized and racialized Canadian Christians. The collection embodies a groundbreaking and a pacesetting attempt to render the once hermeneutically "voiceless visibles" voiceless no more. Such a volume should therefore be warmly welcomed as contributing to the Canadian multi-cultural Christian discourse as we continue to engage in the act of community-creation within the nation of Canada. We do so by, among other things, making provision for new and creative readings of the Bible, the *Grundnorm* or foundational theological document of many Canadians—including its varied ethno-cultural communities—and of the Christian Church as a whole.

15. See Dube and Wafula, eds., *Postcoloniality*; Dube et al., eds., *Postcolonial Perspectives in African*; Dube, "Consuming a Colonial Cultural Bomb, 33–58; Yorke, "United Bible Societies"; Yorke, "Bible Translation"; and Yorke and Renju, *Bible Translation and African Languages*.

9

As One Minoritized Reader to Another

Engaging Biblical Hermeneutics in Canada in the
Twenty-first Century—A Critical Response

GREER ANNE WENH-IN NG

Introduction: All Together in One Place

IN 2009, THE GROUNDBREAKING book *They Were All Together in One Place?* appeared.[1] In it, minoritized biblical scholars and community leaders shared different ways of reading the Bible that were meaningful to their own ethno-cultural communities. This volume provided a much needed space for reflection and dialogue for those of us who, for many years, had been wrestling with how to read the Bible from within our respective communities faithfully and effectively. The volume also became a platform for discussion for those of us who wondered whether these types of readings were even possible at all.

Thinking back, I realize that my own exposure to minoritized groups doing theology together without the "centre" occurred over a decade and a half earlier, with the publication of Justo L. González's *Out of Every Tribe and Nation* in 1992. The book was

1. Bailey et al., eds., *They Were All Together.*

the fruit of a series of face-to-face gatherings of ethnic minority theologians and lay leaders meeting over four years under the sponsorship of the United Methodist Church. The impetus for this sponsorship was the approaching 500th anniversary, in the same year, of the so-called "discovery" of the Americas by Columbus.[2] As an Asian Canadian involved in the project "Christ, Culture, and Community" during approximately the same period, I found myself hugely stimulated and enriched by the theological struggles and discoveries of these leaders from African American, Asian American, Latina/o American, and Native American ecclesial communities. It also happened that the efforts by the Association of Theological Schools of the United States and Canada in introducing and advocating for the "globalization" of theological education took place during some of those years.[3] All this synergy kept the issue alive in my own research, both within the Christ, Culture, and Community project[4] and in anti-racism education later on.[5]

I now realize that my focus at that time was on the need to build alliances among ethno-cultural minoritized groups, an emphasis that might have outweighed an equally important aspect of relationships among such communities, that of dealing with internalized racism and cross-racial hostility. The reminder by the editors of *They Were All Together in One Place?* not to ignore the very real differences in immigration, social, and economic histories as well as ethno-cultural identities is thus also applicable to the efforts of this present volume's endeavor to "read-in-between" by Indigenous, Asian Canadians, African Caribbean Canadians, Indian Canadian, and Latina/o Canadians in the second decade of the twenty-first century.

In her attempt to develop an Asian American biblical hermeneutics, Hebrew Bible scholar Gale A. Yee suggests adopting the criteria posed by W. E. B. Du Bois in 1926 for an authentic Black theatre. As Du Bois puts it, such plays must be (1) About

2. González, *Out of Every Tribe and Nation.*

3. Ng, "Efforts towards the Globalization," 22–26.

4. Ng, "Asian North American Relationships," 229–37.

5. Ng, *That All May Be One.*

us; (2) By us; (3) For us; and (4) Near us.[6] How would it work if we apply similar criteria to non-dominant readings of the Bible such as this volume embodies?

The essays in this volume are definitely *by* minoritized scholars, the fruits of their labor in research and reflection, speaking out of the text of their own lives—their ethno-cultural as well as social identities, scholarly disciplines, social location, and their historical-cultural contexts. However, are they mainly *about* minoritized readers and their communities, ecclesial and beyond? Moreover, whether these readings are specifically *for* minoritized readers is similarly not as certain or well-defined. Although one could say that readers from each specific ethno-cultural community would be best equipped to understand and appreciate what is offered, I suspect and indeed hope that each essay provides any reader of the Bible, regardless of their ethno-cultural background, with new knowledge, stimulating insights, as well as challenging questions that broaden their encounter with Scripture in days to come. Listening to other minoritized voices sometimes requires that those who are readers from ethnically minoritized communities themselves hold back their own traditional worldviews and cultural assumptions. It is true that in many ways, as part of "the rest" as distinct from "the West," we share much that is common among us, but there may also be crucial distinctions.[7]

Hans-Ruedi Weber, a one-time Bible study staff at the World Council of Churches, told the story of an African woman who used to go everywhere carrying a Bible high above her head as she went about her work. When asked why, she declared, "Yes, there are many books which I could read. But there is only one book that reads me."[8] As a minoritized reader, therefore, I am curious as to how the Bible might "read me" even as I follow new ways of how to read it. I am interested in finding ways of how I can engage or be engaged by the Bible via these approaches, exemplified by the narratival hermeneutics this present volume espouses.

6. Yee, "Yin/Yang Is not Me," 156–57.

7. See my exploration in "Salmon and Carp, Bannock and Rice," 197–215.

8. Weber, *Book that Reads Me*, ix.

Indigenous Readings: Translation Matters

Nowhere is the call for engaging and being engaged by the Bible with Du Bois's criteria in mind more urgent than Ray Alfred's passionate plea for rendering the Scriptures accessible to Indigenous communities by Indigenous translators who are steeped in Indigenous worldviews. Alfred points out that, in this task of translating biblical texts into various First Nations languages, it is crucial to equip and train Indigenous biblical scholars to have direct, firsthand access to documents in Hebrew and Greek. Otherwise, as he demonstrates in the rendering of "Anglican" into "white" in Cree, some terms and concepts translated via a dominant lens can be not only inaccurate and misleading but also downright intentionally and dangerously colonizing. Thus, the issue of who has the power to convey an authentic translation becomes more than a linguistic struggle.

To counter this kind of danger, I can think of the efforts made by Chinese biblical scholars in the 1930s in the production of the *Kuoyu* ("national language/vernacular") Bible, still in popular use today. For example, take the "dynamic equivalent" of translating "give us this day our daily bread" in the prayer of Jesus into "give us this day our daily food" (literally "what we drink and eat"). To embed the central idea of this part of the prayer deeply in the receptor culture, nothing else would do for that vast land where "bread" is unfamiliar at best, and where even "rice" or "noodles" alone would not cover the wide variety of regional daily staples.

A much more complex issue pertains to rendering "Logos" in the Prologue to the Gospel of John into *dao* instead of "Word," as in English translations. The term *dao*, literally "way," is a traditional philosophical and cosmological concept familiar to anyone growing up in Chinese culture. For Chinese Christians, it has come to assume a theological significance close to Tillich's understanding of "ultimate" and "ground of being."[9] If we agree

9. The opening two lines of the *Daodejing/Tao Te Ching*, 道 德 經, the scripture of Daoism (founded in the sixth century BC) with authorship ascribed to the sage Laozi 老 子, may be translated thus: The *dao* that can be *daoed*/expressed is not the eternal/constant *dao*; The name that can be named

with Justo Gonzalez that "every translation is an interpretation,"[10] such a culturally specific rendering may strike some mainstream readers as almost a re-interpretation of a concept grounded in Greek thought, adopted and historically accepted by the Christian church. Be that as it may, the fact that this particular rendering of *dao* as an equivalent translation has enabled generations of Chinese Christians to grasp the theological import behind the Evangelist John's Prologue speaks to the power, or even the necessity, of striving to be culturally relevant in the challenging task of translating biblical texts.

Developing Narratival Hermeneutics by and for Latinas/os in Canada

Differences between Latina/o experience in Canada and Latinas/os in the USA experience, as noted by Néstor Medina, renders the development of a distinct Canadian hermeneutics, both *by* and *for*, and where applicable, also *about*, this particular community in Canada especially significant.[11] My fervent hope is that Medina's contribution in the present volume will lead to many more by many other Latina/o Canadians, both to deepen exploration as well as to deal with aspects not able to be covered in this volume (for instance, gender issues).

Before that can happen, as a minoritized reader from outside of this community, I wonder whether there are not sufficient general commonalities to allow for some cross-fertilizing and interpretative sharing between Canadian minoritized communities—for example, between Indigenous communities and Latina/o communities in Canada. A number of years ago, I co-taught a course with the Native Ministries Summer School program at the Vancouver School of Theology. First Nations students were asked

---

is not the eternal/constant name.

10. González, *Out of Every Tribe and Nation*, 57.

11. Here I find most enlightening a comparison of Medina's proposal with Samuel Solivan's account in "Sources of a Hispanic/Latino American Theology," 134–49.

to offer a reading of the Exodus-Joshua story of the Israelites' "entry into Canaan." Whether Giktsan, Nishg'a, or Haida, the class pointed out that their own realities aligned much more closely with the situation of the Canaanites, the invaded, than with the victorious, invading Israelites. Here was a case of interpretation both "by us" and "about us" if ever there was one. These readers arrived at their interpretation independent of being primed by any written or published article on the topic, and definitely before Robert Warrior's brilliant essay on Canaanites, Cowboys, and Indians appeared on the scene.[12]

In an innovative Latina/o American study of Joshua 9, Latina/o readers rendered a "dialogic" account of how the Gibeonites, destined for total extinction by the conquering Israelites, negotiated a modified covenant for their eventual survival, albeit only as enslaved "hewers of wood and drawers of water."[13] This interpretation runs parallel with the Indigenous students at VST, whose territories and communities were similarly invaded and conquered.

As for gender issues in Latina/o biblical interpretation, one wonders whether or to what extent the *mujerista* and *mulata* Christianity approach of Latina/o American theologian Ada María Isasi-Díaz would be helpful for Latinas in Canada. Isasi-Díaz argues for the use of "Bible story as interpretative key" to advocate for identifying a strict "canon within a canon" of liberative texts when tested against Latina American lives.[14] To explore this aspect further might require reflection from *Latina Canadians*, especially if Du Bois's criterion of "by us," is applied.

12. Warrior, "Native American Perspective, 235–41.

13. Garcia-Treto, "Lesson of the Gibeonites, 73–85.

14. Isasi-Díaz, "La Palabra de Dios en Nosotras, 148–69.

Reading at the Interstices: Cross-Textual and Inter-Textual Readings from Asia and the Asian Canadian Diaspora

Living in the interstices of their lives and society,[15] minority readers of Asian heritage in Canada often find themselves, by virtue of necessity, moving away from reading the Bible with what Hong Kong Chinese Hebrew Bible scholar Archie C. C. Lee refers to as the "text-alone approach" or even a "text-context interpretative mode." The expectation is to eventually arrive at what Lee deems to be most helpful in terms of interpretation, i.e., "cross-textual hermeneutics."[16] Lee's study of Chinese creation myths in relation to Genesis is an example of what is possible in this cross-cultural, cross-textual approach.

In the present volume, nowhere is cross-textual hermeneutics better illustrated than in Barbara Leung Lai's *across-the-grain* reading of Ecclesiastes. Leung Lai's metaphor of constructing strong plywood by gluing wood panels perpendicular to one another conjures up a vivid picture of the layers of complex meaning that are made by bringing texts from many sources into relationship (and, indeed, pitting them against one another) with the biblical text—a text already strengthened by its own "cross-grain," complex layers of meaning, as Qohelet's own reflections and statements indicate. Such a reading simultaneously involves traditional Chinese wisdom and Daoist philosophical understandings along with extra-Ecclesiastes biblical thinking. In referencing the life-death choice from Deuteronomy, for instance, Leung Lai offers the kind of personal reflection oriented toward spiritual-growth that Alan Lai identifies as the focus of Bible study for many first-generation Chinese immigrants to Canada.

Similarly, HyeRan Kim-Cragg demonstrates how an "interpositioning" reading from the life texts of theologically trained Korean Canadian women can throw light on the narrative of Jephthah's daughter in Judges 11, lifting up issues not usually dealt with by traditional (i.e., white, majority, and usually male)

---

15. See Brock "Cooking without Recipes," 125–43.

16. Lee, "Biblical Interpretation," 35–39.

interpretations. That her reading is done from both a cross-disciplinary perspective as well as in the context of multifold interpretations of White feminist interpreters attests to the particular contribution such inter-positioning could bring. Thus, a reading based on the political history of this group of readers' homeland, centered on mourning the unjust death of a much-loved, democracy-advocating president, leads them to develop a strategy beyond "mourning as ritual" to "mourning as resistance." At the same time, the stimulus provided by a company of [non-Korean] feminist interpreters pushes them to pursue the whole area of the biblical protagonist's sexuality and what ramifications such pursuit could yield even further. With reference to Du Bois's criteria, the interpretative approach in Kim-Cragg's chapter would seem to satisfy all three: it is definitely done by the group of women doing the reading, it is about them and their home country, and it furthers their biblical understanding as well as their concerns and issues as feminist-oriented women.

By delving into the reading approach and strategy of early twentieth-century Punjabi Christian evangelist Sadhu Sundar Singh (1889–1929), Alison Hari-Singh argues that contemporary Canadian Christians of South Asian heritage, like the Sadhu, continue a form of Christian *bhakti* practice in their own biblical engagement. Following Sundar Singh's contemplative, prayer-focused approach to Bible reading, South Asian readers, especially those from North India, strive to nurture their spirituality and piety effectively by retaining their culturally-inherited approach in defiance of majority-mainline Euro-centric and Euro-North American Western reading norms.[17]

This focus on piety and spiritual enhancement in biblical engagement is shared by the [Evangelical] Chinese Christians in

17. According to R. S. Sugirtharajah's historical categorization of India's three modes of Biblical interpretation, Sadhu Sundar Singh's belongs to the most recent "nativitistic" mode, characterized by the use of vernacular languages and storytelling. This mode follows the colonialist "Anglicist mode," which introduced Western modernist historical critical methods and, in turn, had succeeded the earlier "Orientalist mode," based on Sanskrit and Vedic scholarship. See Sugirtharajah, *Asian Biblical Hermeneutics*, 3–28.

the Canadian diaspora so carefully presented by Alan Lai. No matter what their immigration history or experience, these Christians continue to operate with conscious or unconscious Confucian values. It does make one wonder, however, how they would handle situations in the biblical text when their traditional values are confronted by a different or even contradictory set of values. For instance, how do they reconcile Jesus' belittling of family ties ("Who are my mother and my brothers?" in Mark 3:3–5) with the high priority given to family and family cohesiveness in their traditional culture? Or how do these readers, when faced with the conflict between Jesus' defiance of patriarchal social norms regarding women by associating with women in public, acknowledging women's participation in his public ministry, engaging the Samaritan woman in theological discussion, etc., understand these passages vis-à-vis the patriarchal Confucian injunctions of "three obediences" and "four virtues" for women?[18] In fact, the question "Does Confucius yet live?"[19] could well be asked of "pan-[East]Asian" Canadian Christians (Korean and Vietnamese as well as Chinese) who follow a culturally traditional (that is, Confucian) upbringing, one that has been imbibed and continues to be practiced to a larger or lesser extent depending on their level of conscientization. Such values are so often oppressive toward women.

Looking Forward

As we look forward to continuing the momentum of reading and interpreting the biblical text as minoritized scholars in Canada, it seems to me that several questions might prove to be relevant:

18. My attempt at dealing with these issues can be found in "Asian Sociocultural Values," 63–103.

19. The conclusion of a bilingual survey of twenty Korean churches in New York, New Jersey, and Connecticut was a definite "yes." See Mullinax, "Does Confucius Yet Live?," 28–39.

Where and When Are We Doing These Readings?

Taking the Canadian context seriously, I wish to acknowledge that the nation of Canada, having reached 150 years of confederation (1867–2017), is at this juncture being challenged to re-think its history, a dominant-mainstream official history, which, so far, has neither paid sufficient attention to nor acknowledged alternative accounts of its relationship with its Indigenous communities—First Nations, Métis, and Inuit. As immigrants or children of immigrants (no matter how early or how recent our arrival to this "occupied" treaty land), once we admit to counting ourselves among the oppressing settlers, we must get involved in the recovery of this history, a process that includes un-learning, re-learning, as well as new learning. As members of ethno-cultural minority communities, we must join other non-Indigenous Canadians in responding to the 94 "Calls to Action" arising out of the final report (2015) of the multi-year process of the Truth and Reconciliation Commission on Canada's Indian Residential Schools—institutions of colonization operated on behalf of the Canadian federal government by several major Christian denominations.[20] One of these calls, number 49, asks that faith communities deal with the so-called "Doctrine of Discovery" and notion of *terra nullius*.[21] The kind of impact this un-leaning, re-learning, and new learning may come to assume on our reading of Scripture is yet to be explored. Will hitherto unnoticed or neglected biblical texts jump out at us? Will hitherto accepted interpretations, even in minoritized readings, begin to disturb us? And when they do, how do we make room to not only be engaged by them, but to engage them with respect and courage?

20. For the history and work of this federally appointed commission (2008–2015), see Truth and Reconciliation Commission of Canada, "National Centre for Truth and Reconciliation."

21. See Medina, *On the Doctrine of Discovery*.

Who Is Doing These Readings, and with Whom?

Asian American Hebrew scholar Frank Yamada highlights three aspects of culture: culture is not unified, it deals with power relations, and it is constantly in flux.[22] If this is so, how closely would second and subsequent generations of East Asian Canadians approach the Bible in a way similar to their parents or grandparents who are steeped in the ethos and practice of Confucianism? At the same time, how does a more recent phenomenon—that is, the arrival of a sizable contingent of newcomers to Canada from China finding a place in Chinese Protestant churches—modify the current picture?[23] As for millennials with no religious affiliation, what kind of minimum exposure to the Bible do they wind up with apart from family weddings, funerals, or the occasional Christmas or Easter church service? Would they, instead, be more apt to come across Bible stories in films and TV programs?[24] Finally, as more cross-ethnic and cross-racial couples intermarry, to what extent would the weight slant towards the ethno-cultural majority partner's dominance in society rather than the religious affiliation of the ethno-cultural minoritized partner, even if the latter is strongly religious? How each of these cohorts develop ways of reading the Bible in their own life and in their varied faith communities will probably differ quite significantly from one another.

Where Do Minority Readers Engage the Bible?

As we have seen in the present volume, it would seem more often than not that such readings emerge from and are based not in academic institutions but rather in local faith communities or ecumenical gatherings attended by Christians at a variety of stages of faith development, as well as the occasional seeker or interested

22. Yamada and Guardiola-Saenz, "Culture and Identity," 5.

23. Xu, "Immigrants providing a boost to declining church attendance in Canada."

24. This is the reality presented by Beavis and Kim-Cragg, *What Does the Bible Say?*

unchurched millennials. It will be interesting to watch whether or how these alternative readings "bubble up" to catch the attention of the academy. For that to happen, perhaps "subversive" tactics at the margin of theological disciplines are required, where the fruits of minoritized biblical interpretations can become embedded in practices of ministry in arenas such as homiletics/preaching, religious education, and liturgy/worship.[25]

In the Current Realities of Global Migration, as well as in an Increasingly Intercultural Church, Whether in Europe, Asia, or the Americas, *How Might Minority Christians Learn to Read the Bible "In-between"?*[26]

What kind of influence could the reading strategies of the global south have on their erstwhile compatriots in the Euro-North American diaspora? In a world of migration, of cultures mixing and jostling with one another, "world religions" are at our doorsteps. What kind of influence in scriptural interpretation might different faith communities exert on one another? And how would all of these scriptural understandings interact with current attempts at recovering Indigenous histories and spiritualities?

Concluding Remarks

Moving beyond the "norm" of mainstream readings while acknowledging their usefulness is both necessary and laudable. For minoritized readers like myself, several additional reminders might be worth looking at as we go forward.

First, let us continue to claim the right—indeed, the responsibility—of working out our own readings with fear and trembling,

25. Boyung Lee offers a vision for how this could happen communally in both church and seminary in Lee, *Transforming Congregations through Community*.

26. See the call of Roman Catholic scholars from Belgium in Brazal and Guzman, *Intercultural Church*, and of Canadian Korean and Korean scholars in Kim-Cragg and Choi, *Encounters*.

even at the risk of appearing marginal to the mainstream, as this volume is attempting to do. Only by persisting in such attempts can we hope to continue contributing to the whole.

Second, at the same time, we also need to take the risk of going beyond possible parochialism of our own culture only. As part of this decolonizing attempt, we need to unlearn any stereotypes of minoritized cultures that are not our own. We need to enrich our reading with new perspectives, knowledge, and insights from fellow minoritized readings, as well as allow those to correct our own shortcomings.

Lastly, but most importantly, as a caution against the kind of cultural imperialism that any ethno-cultural minority community has known only too well in their own colonized experience, moving forward, we need to beware of cultural appropriation. To avoid this pitfall, in addition to seeking the permission of those particular cultural communities whose wisdom and cultural symbols we are hoping to cite or incorporate in our own interpretation, we will also need to seek their guidance in how to do it in ways that respect and honor them and, when permission is withheld for whatever reason, to have the grace not to insist. For Far East and other cultures for whom "imitation is the best form of flattery," this will not be an easy lesson to learn, but it is a necessary one. Until we are willing to practice such an attitude, it may not be possible to be "all together in one place," with integrity and faithfulness, without oppressing one another.

Bibliography

Álvarez, Carmelo E. "Lo popular: Clave hermenéutica del movimiento pentecostal." In *Pentecostalismo y liberación: Una experiencia latino-americana*, edited by Carmelo E. Álvarez, 89–100. Costa Rica: Departamento Ecuménico de Investigaciones, 1992.

Anderson, Herbert. "Violent Death, Public Tragedy, And Rituals of Lament: An Interfaith Agenda." In *Ordo: Bath, Word, Prayer, Table. A Liturgical Primer in Honor of Gordon W. Lathrop*, edited by Dirk G. Lange and Dwight W. Vogel, 188–200. Akron, OH: OSL, 2005.

Appasamy, A. J. *Sundar Singh*. London: Lutterworth, 2002.

Archer, Kenneth J. *A Pentecostal Hermeneutic for the Twenty-First Century: Spirit, Scripture, and Community*. Journal of Pentecostal Theology Supplement Series. London: T. & T. Clark, 2004.

Assmann, Jan. *Religion and Cultural Memory: Ten Studies*. Stanford: Stanford University Press, 2006.

Austin, A., and J. S. Scott. *Canadian Missionaries, Indigenous Peoples: Representing Religion at Home and Abroad*. Toronto: University of Toronto Press, 2005.

Bailey, Randall C., et al., eds. *They Were All Together in One Place? Toward Minority Biblical Criticism*. Semeia Studies. Atlanta: Society of Biblical Literature, 2009.

Bakhtin, Mikhael M. *The Dialogic Imagination: Four Essays*. Edited and translated by Caryl Emerson and Michael Holquist. Austin, TX: University of Texas Press, 1986.

Bal, Mieke. *Death and Dissymmerty: The Politics of Coherence in the Book of Judges*. Chicago: University of Chicago Press, 1988.

Bartholomew, Craig G. *Ecclesiastes*. Baker Commentary on the Old Testament: Wisdom and Psalms. Grand Rapids: Baker Academic, 2009.

Basham, Arthur L. *The Origins and Development of Classical Hinduism*. Edited by Kenneth Zysk. New York: Oxford University Press, 1991.

Beavis, Mary Ann. "A Daughter in Israel: Celebrating *Bat Jephthah* (Judg 11:39d–40)." *Feminist Theology: The Journal of the Britain & Ireland School of Feminist Theology* 13 (2004) 11–25.

———. "The Resurrection of Jephthah's Daughter: Judges 11:34–40 and Mark 5:21–24, 35–43." *Catholic Biblical Quarterly* 72 (2010) 46–62.

Berlin, Adele. *Poetics and Interpretation of Biblical Narrative.* Winona Lake, IN: Eisenbrauns, 1994.

Bhabha, Homi K. *The Location of Culture.* New York: Routledge, 1994.

Blount, Brian, et al., eds. *True to Our Native Land: An African American New Testament Commentary.* Minneapolis: Fortress, 2007.

Blumenthal, David R. *Facing an Abusing God: A Theology of Protest.* Louisville: Westminster John Knox, 1993.

Boer, Roland, and Fernando Segovia, eds. *The Future of the Biblical Past: Envisioning Biblical Studies on a Global Key.* Atlanta: Society of Biblical Literature, 2012.

Boesak, Allan, and Curtiss Young. *Radical Reconciliation: Beyond Political Pietism and Christian Quietism.* Maryknoll, NY: Orbis, 2012.

Bohmbach, Karla G. *Women in Scripture: A Dictionary of Named and Unnamed Women in the Hebrew Bible, the Apocryphal/Deuterocannonical Books, and the New Testament,* edited by Carol Meyers. New York: Houghton Mifflin, 2000.

Boyd, Robin. *An Introduction to Indian Christian Theology.* Delhi: ISPCK, 2000.

Boys, Mary C. *Has God Only One Blessing: Judaism as a Source of Christian Self Understanding.* Mahwah, NJ: Paulist, 2000.

Braun, Willi. "Socio-Rhetorical Interests: Context." In *Whose Historical Jesus?,* edited by William Arnal and Michel Desjardins, 92–97. Studies in Christianity and Judaism 7. Waterloo, ON: Wilfrid Laurier University Press, 1997.

Brazal, Agnes M., and Emmanuel S. de Guzman. *Intercultural Church: Bridge of Solidarity in the Migration Context.* n.p.: Borderless, 2015.

Brown, John, and Mick Cooper, eds. *The Plural Self: Multiplicity in Everyday Life.* Thousand Oaks, CA: Sage, 1999.

Browning, Robert, and Roy A. Reed. *The Sacraments in Religious Education and Liturgy.* Birmingham, AL: Religious Education, 1985.

Bryce Bjork, Patrick. *The Novels of Toni Morrison: The Search for Self and Place within the Community.* American University Studies. Series XXIV, American Literature 31. New York: Lang, 1992.

Butler, Judith. *Gender Trouble: Feminism and the Subversion of Identity.* New York: Routledge, 1990.

Callero, Peter L. "The Society of the Self." *Annual Review of Sociology* 29 (2003) 115–33.

Campos, Bernardo L. "Lo testimonial: Un caso de teología oral y narrativa." In *Pentecostalismo y liberación: Una experiencia latinoamericana,* edited by Carmelo E. Álvarez, 125–46. Costa Rica: Departamento Ecuménico de Investigaciones, 1992.

Chao, Jonathan. "The Gospel and Culture in Chinese History." In *Chinese Intellectuals and the Gospel*, edited by Samuel Ling and Stacey Bieler, 9–14. Phillipsburg, NJ: P&R, 1999.

Charleston, Steven. "Reflections on a Revival: The Native American Alternative." *Theological Education* 20 (1983) 65–78.

Christianson, Eric S. *A Time to Tell: Narrative Strategies in Ecclesiastes.* JSOTSup 280. Sheffield: Sheffield Academic, 1998.

Chu, Patricia. *Assimilating Asians: Gendered Strategies of Authorship in Asian America.* Durham: Duke University Press, 2000.

Chung, David. *Syncretism: The Religious Context of Christian Beginnings in Korea.* Albany: SUNY Press, 2001.

Committee of Reference and Counsel of the Foreign Missions Conference of North America. *Christian Education in China: A Study Made by an Educational Commission Representing the Mission Boards and Societies Conducting Work in China.* New York: Foreign Missions Conference, 1922.

Cox, James L. *The Impact of Christian Missions on Indigenous Cultures: The Real People and the Unreal Gospel.* Lewiston, NY: Mellen, 1991.

Cuellar, Gregory. "The Task of Decentering in Teaching Old Testament." Wabash Center. 20 August 2015. https://www.wabashcenter.wabash.edu/author/gregory-cuellar.

Davis, Casey Wayne. *Oral Biblical Criticism: The Influence of the Principles of Orality on the Literary Structure of Paul's Epistle to the Philippians.* JSNTSup 172. Sheffield: Sheffield Academic, 1999.

Day, Peggy L. "From the Child Is Born the Woman: The Story of Jephthah's Daughter." In *Gender and Difference in Ancient Israel*, edited by Peggy L. Day, 58–74. Minneapolis: Fortress, 1989.

Donaldson, Laura. *Decolonizing Feminisms: Race, Gender, and Empire-Building.* Chapel Hill: University of North Carolina Press, 1992.

Dube, Musa. "Consuming a Colonial Cultural Bomb: Translating Badimo into 'Demons' in the Setswana Bible (Matthew 8:28–34; 15:22; 10:8)." *Journal for the Study of the New Testament* 21/73 (1999) 33–58.

———. *Postcolonial Feminist Interpretation of the Bible.* St. Louis: Chalice, 2000.

Dube, Musa, et al., eds. *Postcolonial Perspectives in African Biblical Interpretations.* Global Perspectives on Biblical Scholarship 13. Atlanta: Society of Biblical Literature, 2012.

Dube, Musa, and Robert Wafula, eds. *Postcoloniality, Translation, and the Bible in Africa.* Eugene, OR: Pickwick Publications, 2017.

Erskine, Noel. *Plantation Church: How African American Religion was Born in Caribbean Slavery.* Oxford: Oxford University Press, 2014.

Exum, J. Cheryl. "Murder They Wrote: Ideology and the Manipulation of Female Presence in Biblical Narrative." In *The Pleasure of Her Text: Feminist Readings of Biblical and Historical Texts*, edited by Alice Bach, 45–67. Philadelphia: Trinity, 1990.

————. "Tragic Vision and Biblical Narrative." In *Signs and Wonders: Biblical Texts in Literary Focus*, edited by Cheryl Exum, 59–84. Semeia Studies. Atlanta: Society of Biblical Literature, 1989.

Felder, Cain Hope, ed. *Stony the Road We Trod: African American Biblical Interpretation.* Minneapolis: Fortress, 1991.

————. *Troubling Biblical Waters: Race, Class and Family.* Maryknoll, NY: Orbis, 1989.

Fetzer, Anita, and Etsuko Oishi, eds. *Context and Contexts.* Philadelphia: Benjamins, 2011.

Fewell, Danna Nolan. "Judges." In *Women's Bible Commentary,* edited by Carol A. Newsom and Sharon H. Ringe, 67–78. Louisville: Westminster John Knox, 1998.

Flood, Gavin. *Introduction to Hinduism.* New York: Cambridge University Press, 1996.

Fox, Michael. "Frame-Narrative and Composition in the Book of Qohelet." *Hebrew Union College Annual* 48 (1997) 83–106.

Francis, T. Dayanandan. *Sadhu Sundar Singh: The Lover of the Cross.* Madras: Christian Literature Society, 1989.

Friesen, John W. *Aboriginal Spirituality and Biblical Theology: Closer Than You Think.* Calgary: Detselig Enterprises, 2000.

Fuchs, Esther. *Sexual Politics in the Biblical Narrative: Reading the Hebrew Bible as a Woman.* JSOTSup 310. Sheffield: Sheffield Academic, 2000.

Gadamer, Hans-Georg. *Truth and Method.* Translated by Garret Barden and John Cumming. New York: Seabury, 1975.

García-Treto, Francisco O. "The Lesson of the Gibeonites: A Proposal for Dialogic Attention as a Strategy for Reading the Bible." In *Hispanic/Latino Theology: Challenge and Promise,* edited by Ada María Isasi-Díaz and Fernando Segovia, 73–85. Minneapolis: Fortress, 1996.

Gerstein, Beth. "A Ritual Processed: A Look at Judges 11:40." In *Anti-Covenant: Counter-Reading Women's Lives in the Hebrew Bible,* edited by Mieke Bal, 175–93. JSOTSup 81. Sheffield: Almond, 1989.

Ginieniewicz, Jorge. "Political Participation of Latin Americans in Canada: What Do We Know So Far?" In *Ruptures, Continuities, and Re-Learning: The Political Participation of Latin Americans in Canada,* edited by Jorge Ginieniewicz and Daniel Schugurensky, 34–45. Toronto: OISE/UT, 2006

Goldingay, John. *Old Testament Theology.* 3 vols. Downers Grove, IL: InterVarsity, 2003–2009.

González, Justo L. *Out of Every Tribe and Nation: Christian Theology at the Ethnic Roundtable.* Nashville: Abingdon, 1992.

————. "Worship and Fiesta." In *Primary Sources in Liturgical Theology,* edited by Dwight W. Vogel, 255–60. Collegeville, MN: Liturgical, 2000.

Government of Canada. "Georges Philias Vanier." Vanier Canada Graduate Scholarships. 25 June 2014. http://www.vanier.gc.ca/en/georges_vanier.html.

Green, Joel B., and Max Turner. *Between Two Horizons: Spanning New Testament Studies and Systematic Theology.* Grand Rapids: Eerdmans, 2000.

Greenwood, Kyle R. "Debating Wisdom: The Role of Voice in Ecclesiastes." *Catholic Biblical Quarterly* 74 (2012) 476–91.

Grouard, Émile. *The Beginning of Print Culture in Athabasca Country: A Facsimile Edition & Translation of a Prayer Book in Cree Syllabics.* Translated by Patricia Demers, et al. Edmonton: University of Alberta Press, 2010.

Han, Kuk-Yom. "Mariology as a Base for Feminist Liberation Theology." In *Asian Women Doing Theology: Report from Singapore Conference,* edited by Dulcie Abraham, et al., 234–40. Hong Kong: Asian Women's Resource Centre for Culture and Theology, 1989.

Haque, Eve. *Multiculturalism within a Bilingual Framework: Language, Race, and Belonging in Canada.* Toronto: University of Toronto Press, 2012.

Harrington, Daniel J. "Pseudo-Philo." In *The Old Testament Pseudepigrapha,* edited by James H. Charlesworth, 2:297–377. Garden City, NY: Doubleday, 1985.

Hedlund, Roger. "India's New Era of World Christianity in the 21st Century." In *Roswith Gerloff, Auf Grenzen—Ein Leben im Dazwischen van Kulturen,* edited by Armin Triebel, 225–37. Berlin: Weissensee, 2016.

Heiler, Friedrich. *The Gospel of Sadhu Sundar Singh.* Translated by Olive Wyon. New York: Oxford University Press, 1927.

Hinnenkamp, Katie. "*Justicia* for Migrant Workers: In Search of a Guestworker Program by the Workers, for the Workers." In *Ruptures, Continuities and Re-Learning: The Political Participation of Latin Americans in Canada,* edited by Jorge Ginieniewicz and Daniel Schugurensky, 148–53. Toronto: OISE/UT, 2006.

Hollenweger, Walter J. *El pentecostalismo: Historia y doctrina.* Buenos Aires: La Aurora, 1976.

Holmstedt, Robert D. "אני ולבי: The Syntactic Encoding of the Collaborative Nature of Qohelet's Experiment." *Journal of Hebrew Scriptures* 9 (2010) 1–27.

Hopkins, Thomas J. "Bhakti Hinduism." In *The Perennial Dictionary of World Religions,* edited by Keith Crim, et al., 99. San Francisco: Harper&Row, 1989.

Horden, John. "A Cree Pastoral by the First Bishop of Moosonee." Translated and edited by R. B. Horsefield. *Journal of the Canadian Church Historical Society* 5.2 (1963).

Hsu, Francis L. K. "The Self in Cross-Cultural Perspective." In *Culture and Self: Asian and Western Perspectives,* edited by Anthony J. Marsella, et al., 24–55. Social Science Paperbacks 280. New York: Tavistock, 1985.

Isasi-Díaz, Ada María. *Mujerista Theology.* Maryknoll, NY: Orbis, 1996.

John Paul II. "Redemptoris Missio: On the Permanent Validity of the Church's Missionary Mandate." http://w2.vatican.va/content/john-paul-ii/en/encyclicals/documents/hf_jp-ii_enc_07121990_redemptoris-missio.pdf.

Kaiser, Sigurd. "Church Growth in China: Some Observations from an Ecumenical Perspective." *Ecumenical Review* 67 (2015) 35–47.

Kim, Nami. "My/Our Comfort Not at the Expense of Somebody Else's: Toward a Critical Global Feminist Theology." *Journal of Feminist Studies in Religion* 21.2 (2005) 75–94.

Kim-Cragg, HyeRan. "Becoming a Feminist Christian: A Korean-Canadian Perspective." In *My Red Couch and Other Stories on Seeking a Feminist Faith*, edited by Claire Bischoff and Rachel Gaffron, 183–89. Cleveland: Pilgrim, 2005.

———. "Holy Week: Heart of the Universe: Healing All." In *Rising with the Morning Star: Daily Reflections for Lent*, edited by Betty Lynn Schwab, 95–112. Toronto: United Church, 2011.

———. *Story and Song: A Postcolonial Interplay between Christian Education and Worship*. American University Studies. Series VII, Theology and Religion 323. New York: Lang, 2012.

Kim-Cragg, HyeRan, and Eun Young Choi. *The Encounters: Retelling the Bible from Migration and Intercultural Perspectives*. Translated by Lark Kim. Daejeon: Daejanggang, 2013.

Kitagawa, Joseph Mitsuo. *The Christian Tradition: Beyond its European Captivity*. Philadelphia: Trinity, 1992.

Kwok, Pui-lan. *Postcolonial Imagination and Feminist Theology*. Louisville: Westminster John Knox, 2005.

Lai, Alan Ka Lun. "Where Are Asian Christians in Jewish-Christian Dialogue?" *Consensus* 32.1 (2007) 79–94.

Lai, David Chuenyan, et al. "The Chinese in Canada: Their Unrecognized Religion." In *Religion and Ethnicity in Canada*, edited by Paul Bramadat and David Seljak, 89–110. Toronto: Pearson Education Canada, 2005.

Lai, John C. "Andragogy of the Oppressed: Emancipatory Education for Christian Adults." The Education Resources Information Center, 1995. http://www.lindenwood.edu/education/andragogy/andragogy/2011/Lai_1995.pdf.

Lala, Chhaganlal. *Philosophy of Bhakti*. Delhi: South Asia, 1990.

Landy, Frances. "The Impersonal Voice in First-Person Narrative Fiction." *Narrative* 12 (2004) 113–51.

———. "Vision and Voice in Isaiah." *Journal for the Study of the Old Testament* 88 (2000) 19–36.

Latourette, Kenneth Scott. *A History of Chinese Missions in China*. New York: Macmillan, 1929.

LeBlanc, Terry. "Residential School: Policy, Power, and Mission." In *Edinburgh 2010: Mission Today and Tomorrow*, 90–94. Eugene, OR: Wipf & Stock, 2011.

Lee, Archie C. C. "The Bible in Chinese Christianity: Its Reception and Appropriation in China." *Ecumenical Review* 67.1 (2015) 96–106.

———. "Biblical Interpretation in Asian Perspectives." *Asia Journal of Theology* 7.1 (1993) 35–39.

Lee, Boyung. *Transforming Congregations through Community: Faith Formation from the Seminary to the Church*. Louisville: Westminster John Knox, 2013.

Lee, Jung Young. *Marginality: The Key to Multicultural Theology*. Minneapolis: Fortress, 1995.

Lee, Kyung-Sook. *The Women in Hebrew Scripture*. Seoul: Korean Christian Literature Society, 1994.

Lerner, Gerda. *The Creation of Patriarchy*. New York: Oxford University Press, 1986.

Leung Lai, Barbara M. "The Preacher and One's Own Text-of-life." In *Global Perspectives on the Old Testament*, edited by Mark Roncace and Joseph Weaver, 214–16. Upper Saddle River, NJ: Pearson, 2014.

———. "Psalm 44 and the Function of Lament and Protest." *Old Testament Essays* 20 (2007) 418–31.

———. *Through the "I"-Window: The Inner Life of Characters in the Hebrew Bible*. Hebrew Bible Monographs 34. Sheffield: Sheffield Phoenix, 2011.

———. "Voice and Ideology in Ecclesiastes: Reading 'Cross the Grains." In *Interested Readers: Essays on the Hebrew Bible in Honor of David J. A. Clines*, edited by James K. Aitken, et al., 265–78. Atlanta: SBL Press, 2013.

Li, Peter S. *Chinese in Canada*. 2nd ed. Toronto: Oxford University Press, 1998.

Liew, Tat-siong Benny. "Queering Closets and Perverting Desires: Cross-Examining John's Engendering and Transgendering Word across Different Worlds." In *They Were All Together in One Place: Toward Minority Biblical Criticism*, edited by Randall C. Bailey, et al., 251–88. Semeia Studies 57. Atlanta: Society of Biblical Literature, 2009.

Lindbeck, George A. *The Nature of Doctrine: Religion and Theology in a Port-Liberal Age*. Louisville: Westminster John Knox, 1984.

Litchfield, Randy G. "Rethinking Local Bible Study in a Postmodern Era." In *New Paradigms for Bible Study: The Bible in the Third Millennium*, edited by Robert Fowler, et al., 227–50. New York: T. & T. Clark, 2004.

Lodwick, Kathleen. *Crusaders against Opium: Protestant Missionaries in China, 1874–1917*. Lexington: University Press of Kentucky, 1996.

Long, John S. "John Horden, First Bishop of Moosonee: Diplomat and Man of Compromise." *Journal of the Canadian Church Historical Society* 27.2 (1985) 86–97.

Malhotra, Rajiv. *Being Different*. Delhi: HarperCollins India, 2011.

Manuel, George, and Michael Posluns. *The Fourth World: An Indian Reality*. New York: Free Press, 1974.

Maxey, James A. *Orality to Orality: A New Paradigm for Contextual Translation of the Bible*. Biblical Performance Criticism Series 2. Eugene, OR: Cascade Books, 2009.

McCall, Sophie. "'What the Map Cuts up, the Story Cuts Across': Translating Oral Traditions and Aboriginal Land Title." *Essays on Canadian Writing* 80 (2003) 305–28.

McLeod, Neal. *Cree Narrative Memory: From Treaties to Contemporary Times*. Saskatoon: Purich, 2007.

Medina, Néstor. "Being Church as Latina/o Pentecostals." In *Church in an Age of Global Migration: A Moving Body*, edited by Susanna Snyder, et al., 65–82. Pathways for Ecumenical and Interreligious Dialogue Series. New York: Palgrave MacMillan, 2015.

———. *On the Doctrine of Discovery*. Toronto: Canadian Council of Churches, 2017.

———. "Orality and Context in a Hermeneutical Key: Toward a Latina/o Canadian Pentecostal Life-Narrative Hermeneutics." *PentecosStudies* 14.1 (2015) 97–123.

———. "Reflections of a Snow Mexican: Immigration, Canada and the Northern Border." Paper presented at Theology Beyond Borders: Political Borders, Human Crisis, and Religion. American Academy of Religion. San Antonio, TX, 20 November 2016.

———. *Truth and Reconciliation and the Doctrine of Discovery: Select Responses of Member Denominations*. Toronto: Canadian Council of Churches, 2017.

Mercer, Joyce Ann. "Interdisciplinarity as a Practical Theological Conundrum." In *Conundrum in Practical Theology*, edited by Joyce Ann Mercer and Bonnie J. Miller-McLemore, 163–89. Leiden: Brill, 2016.

Míguez Bonino, José. *Rostros del protestantismo latinoamericano*. Grand Rapids: Nueva Creación, 1995.

Miller, Barbara. *Tell It On the Mountain: The Daughter of Jephthah in Judges 11*. Interfaces Series. Collegeville, MN: Liturgical, 2005.

Mitchell, Katharyne. "Different Diasporas and the Hype of Hybridity." *Environment and Planning D: Society and Space* 5.5 (1997) 533–53.

Moffett, Samuel Hugh. *Beginnings to 1500*. Vol 1. of *A History of Christianity in Asia*. San Francisco: HarperSanFrancisco, 1992.

Moore, Charles E. "Introduction." *Sadhu Sundar Singh: Essential Writings*, edited by Charles E. Moore, 9–30. Maryknoll, NY: Orbis, 2005.

Moore, Stephen, and Fernando Segovia, eds. *Postcolonial Biblical Criticism: Interdisciplinary Intersections*. Bible and Postcolonialism. London: T. & T. Clark, 2005.

Moy, Russell. "American Racism: The Null Curriculum in Religious Education." *Religious Education* 95 (2000) 121–25.

Mullinax, Marc S. "Does Confucius Yet Live? Answers from Korean American Churches." *Journal of Asian and Asian American Theology* 3.1 (1999) 28–39.

Murphy, Roland E. *Ecclesiastes*. Word Biblical Commentary 23. Dallas: Word, 1992.

Nakashima Brock, Rita. "Cooking without Recipes: Interstitial Integrity." In *Off the Menu: Asian and Asian North American Women's Religion and Theology*, edited by Rita Nakashima Brock, et al., 125–43. Louisville: Westminster John Knox, 2007.

Neumann, Peter D. *Pentecostal Experience: An Ecumenical Encounter*. Princeton Theological Monograph Series 187. Eugene, OR: Pickwick Publications, 2012.

Newbigin, Lesslie. *Foolishness to the Greeks: The Gospel and Western Culture.* Grand Rapids: Eerdmans, 1986.

Newsom, Carol A. "Reflections on Ideological Criticism and Postcritical Perspectives." In *Method Matters: Essays on the Interpretation of the Hebrew Bible in Honor of David L. Petersen,* edited by Joel M. LeMon and Kent Harold Richards, 553–57. SBL Resources for Biblical Studies 56. Atlanta: Society of Biblical Literature, 2009.

Ng, Greer Anne Wenh-In. "Asian North American Relationships with Other Minority Cultures." In *People on the Way: Asian North Americans Discovering Christ, Culture, and Community,* edited by David Ng, 229–37. Valley Forge, PA: Judson, 1996.

———. "Asian Sociocultural Values: Oppressive and Liberating Aspects from a Woman's Perspective." In *People on the Way: Asian North Americans Discovering Christ, Culture, and Community,* edited by David Ng, 63–103. Valley Forge, PA: Judson, 1996.

———. "Efforts towards the Globalization of Theological Education in the Association of Theological Schools of the United States and Canada." *Ministerial Formation* 70 (1995) 22–26.

———. "Pacific-Asian North American Religious Education." In *Multicultural Religious Education,* edited by Barbara Wilkerson, 190–234. Birmingham, AL: Religious Education, 1997.

———. "Salmon and Carp, Bannock and Rice: Solidarity between Asian Canadian Women and Aboriginal Women." In *Off the Menu: Asian and Asian North American Women's Religion and Theology,* edited by Rita Nakashima Brock, et al., 197–215. Louisville: Westminster John Knox, 2007.

———. *That All May Be One: A Resource for Educating toward Racial Justice.* Toronto: United Church, 2004.

Olson, Dennis T. "The Book of Judges." In *The New Interpreter's Bible,* edited by Leander E. Keck, 2:721–888. Nashville: Abingdon, 1998.

Ong, Walter J. *Orality and Literacy: The Technologizing of the Word.* New York: Routledge, 2002.

Page, Hugh, ed. *Reading Israel's Scriptures in Africa and in the African Diaspora.* Minneapolis: Fortress, 2010.

Palmer, Delano. *Messianic "I", Rastafari and the New Testament in Dialogue.* Lanham, MD: University Press of America, 2010.

Parry, Benita. "Problems in Current Theories of Colonial Discourse." In *The Post-Colonial Studies Reader,* edited by Bill Ashcroft, Gareth Griffiths, and Helen Tiffin, 44–51. London: Routledge, 1995.

Pechilis Prentiss, Karen. *Embodiment of Bhakti.* New York: Oxford University Press, 1999.

Procter-Smith, Marjorie. *In Her Own Rite: Constructing Feminist Liturgical Tradition.* Nashville: Abingdon, 1990.

Ricoeur, Paul. *Interpretation Theory: Discourse and the Surplus of Meaning.* Fort Worth, TX: Texas Christian University Press, 1976.

Rodrigues, Hillary. *Introducing Hinduism*. New York: Routledge, 2006.

Saad, Samia. "The Cost of Invisibility: The Psychosocial Impact of Falling Out of Status." In *Producing and Negotiating Non-Citizenship: Precarious Legal Status in Canada*, edited by Luin Goldring and Patricia Landolt, 137–54. Toronto: University of Toronto Press, 2013.

Schiffrin, Deborah. "Narrative as Self-Portrait: Sociolinguistic Construction of Identity." *Language in Society* 25.2 (1996) 167–203.

Schüssler Fiorenza, Elisabeth. *Democratizing Biblical Studies: Toward an Emancipatory Educational Space*. Louisville: Westminster John Knox, 2009.

Segovia, Fernando F. *Decolonizing Biblical Studies: A View from the Margins*. Maryknoll, NY: Orbis, 2000.

Sepúlveda, Juan. "Pentecostalism as Popular Religiosity." *International Review of Mission* 78.309 (1989) 80–88.

Sharma, Arvind. "Hinduism." In *Our Religions: The Seven World Religions Introduced by Preeminent Scholars from Each Tradition*, edited by Arvind Sharma, 1–68. New York: HarperSanFrancisco, 1983.

Shead, Andrew G. "Reading Ecclesiastes 'Epilogically.'" *Tyndale Bulletin* 48 (1997) 86–91.

Shreve, Dorothy A. *The AfriCanadian Church: A Stabilizer*. St. Catherines, ON: Paideia, 1983.

Simon, Roger. *The Touch of the Past: Remembrance, Learning, and Ethics*. New York: Palgrave Macmillan, 2005.

Singh, R. Raj. *Bhakti and Philosophy*. Lanham, MD: Lexington, 2006.

Smith, Mitzi, ed. *I Found God in Me: A Womanist Biblical Hermeneutics Reader*. Eugene, OR: Cascade Books, 2015.

Smith-Christopher, Daniel, ed. *Text and Experience: Toward a Cultural Exegesis of the Bible*. Biblical Seminar 35. Sheffield: Sheffield Academic, 1995.

Snodgrass, Klyne. "Reading to Hear: A Hermeneutics of Hearing." *Horizons in Biblical Theology* 24 (2002) 1–32.

Solivan, Samuel. "Sources of a Hispanic/Latino American Theology: A Pentecostal Perspective." In *Hispanic/Latino Theology: Challenge and Promise*, edited by Ada Maria Isasi-Díaz and Fernando F. Segovia, 134–49. Minneapolis: Fortress, 1996.

Soulen, R. Kendall. *The God of Israel and Christian Theology*. Minneapolis: Fortress, 1996.

Spence, Jonathan D. "Matteo Ricci and the Ascent to Peking." In *East Meets West: The Jesuits in China, 1582–1773*, edited by Charles E. Ronan and Bonnie B. C. Oh, 3–18. Chicago: Loyola University Press, 1988.

Statistics Canada. "The Latin American Community in Canada." http://www.statcan.gc.ca/pub/89-621-x/89-621-x2007008-eng.htm.

Streeter, B. J., and A. J. Appasamy. *The Message of Sadhu Sundar Singh*. New York: Macmillan, 1921.

Sugirtharajah, R. S. *Asian Biblical Hermeneutics and Postcolonialism: Contesting the Interpretations*. Maryknoll, NY: Orbis, 1998.

Szmulewicz, Esteban, Mónica López, and Duberlis Ramos. "How Is Canada Looking at the Latin-American Immigration: A Backgrounder." Toronto: Hispanic Development Council, 2007.

Thatcher, Tom. "Why John Wrote a Gospel: Memory and History in Early Christianity." In *Memory, Tradition, and Text: Uses of the Past in Early Christian Studies*, edited by Alan Kirk and Tom Thatcher, 79–98. Semeia Studies 52. Atlanta: Society of Biblical Literature, 2005.

Thiselton, Anthony C. *New Horizons in Hermeneutics*. London: HarperCollins, 1992.

Tinker, George E. *Spirit and Resistance: Political Theology and American Indian Liberation*. Minneapolis: Fortress, 2004.

Trible, Phyllis. *Texts of Terror: Literary-Feminist Readings of Biblical Narratives*. Overtures to Biblical Theology. Philadelphia: Fortress, 1984.

Trinh, Minh-Ha. *Women, Native, Other: Writing Postcoloniality and Feminism*. Bloomington: Indiana University Press, 1989.

Truth and Reconciliation Commission of Canada. *Honouring the Truth, Reconciling for the Future: Summary of the Final Report of the Truth and Reconciliation Commission of Canada*. Ottawa: Truth and Reconciliation Commission of Canada, 2015. http://www.trc.ca/websites/trcinstitution/File/2015/Findings/Exec_Summary_2015_05_31_web_o.pdf.

Truth and Reconciliation Commission of Canada. "National Centre for Truth and Reconciliation." http://www.trc.ca/websites/trcinstitution/index.php.

Tu, Wei-Ming. *Humanity and Self-Cultivation: Essays in Confucian Thought*. Boston: Cheng & Tsui, 1998.

van Wolde, Ellen. "Intertextuality: Ruth in Dialogue with Tamar." In *A Feminist Companion to Reading the Bible: Approaches, Methods and Strategies*, edited by Athalya Brenner and Carole Fontaine, 426–51. Feminist Companion to the Bible 11. Sheffield: Sheffield Academic, 1997.

Vandervelde, Pol. *The Task of the Interpreter: Text, Meaning, and Negotiation*. Pittsburgh: University of Pittsburgh Press, 2005.

Vikner, David L. "Lessons from the Church in China." *Currents in Theology and Mission* 17 (1990) 367–74.

Vondey, Wolfgang. *Beyond Pentecostalism: The Crisis of Global Christianity and the Renewal of the Theological Agenda*. Grand Rapids: Eerdmans, 2010.

Walton, Timothy. "Reading Qohelet as Text, Author, and Reader." In *Tradition and Innovation in Biblical Interpretation: Studies Presented to Professor Eep Talstra on the Occasion of his Sixty-Fifth Birthday*, edited by W. Th. Van Peursen and J. W. Dyk, 113–32. Studia Semitica Neerlandica 57. Leiden: Brill, 2011.

Watkins, E. A. *A Dictionary of the Cree Language, as Spoken by the Indians of the Hudson's Bay Company's Territories*. London: SPCK, 1865.

Warrior, Robert Allen. "A Native American Perspective: Canaanites, Cowboys, and Indians." In *Voices from the Margin: Interpreting the Bible in the Third World*, edited by R. S. Sugirtharajah, 235–41. Maryknoll, NY: Orbis, 2006.

Weber, Hans-Ruedi. *The Book that Reads Me: A Handbook for Bible Study Enablers.* Geneva: WCC Publications, 1995.

Werbner, Richard. "Introduction: Multiple Identities, Plural Arenas." In *Postcolonial Identities in Africa*, edited by Richard Werbner and Terence Ranger, 1–25. London: Zed, 1996.

West, Gerald. *The Stolen Bible: From Tool of Imperialism to African Icon.* Biblical Interpretation Series 144. Leiden: Brill, 2016.

Wikipedia. "Bell of King Seongdeok." https://en.wikipedia.org/wiki/Bell_of_King_Seongdeok.

Xu, Xiao. "Immigrants Providing a Boost to Declining Church Attendance in Canada." *The Globe and Mail.* 22 December 2017. https://www.theglobeandmail.com/news/british-columbia/immigrants-providing-a-boost-to-declining-church-attendance-in-canada/article37423409.

Yamada, Frank M., and Leticia A. Guardiola-Saenz. "Culture and Identity." In *The Peoples' Companion to the Bible: New Revised Standard Version, with Apocrypha*, edited by Curtiss Paul DeYoung, et al., 3–9. Minneapolis: Fortress, 2010.

Yang, Fenggang. *Chinese Christians in America: Conversion, Assimilation, and Adhesive Identities.* University Park: Pennsylvania State University Press, 1999.

Yee, Gale A. "Yin/Yang Is not Me: An Exploration into an Asian American Biblical Hermeneutics." In *Ways of Being, Ways of Reading: Asian American Biblical Interpretation*, edited by Mary F. Foskett and Jeffrey Kah-Jin Kuan, 152–63. St. Louis: Chalice, 2006.

Yonhap News. "History and Legend of Emille Bell." http://www.markinsamerica.com/MA5/emille.php.

Yoo, Yani. "Han-Laden Women: Korean 'Comfort Women' and Women in Judges 19–21." *Semeia* 78 (1997) 37–46.

Yorke, Gosnell L. "AfriCanadian Theology: A Newcomer." *African Methodist Episcopal Zion Quarterly Review* 5.98 (1986) 1–12.

———. "Bible Translation in Anglophone Africa and Her Diaspora: A Postcolonialist Agenda." *Black Theology: An International Journal* 2.2 (2004) 153–66.

———. "Blacks and the Bible." In *The Bible in Africa: Transactions, Trajectories and Trends*, edited by Gerald West and Musa Dube, 127–149. Leiden: Brill, 2000.

———. "Foreword." In *A Kairos Moment for Caribbean Theology: Ecumenical Voices in Dialogue*, edited by Garnett Roper and Richard Middleton, ix–xi. Eugene, OR: Pickwick Publications, 2013.

———. "Foreword." In *Teaching All Nations: Interrogating the Matthean Great Commission*, edited by Mitzi Smith and Jayachitra Lalitha, xiii–xiv. Minneapolis: Fortress, 2014.

———. "The United Bible Societies." In *Encyclopedia of Caribbean Religions*, edited by Patrick Taylor and Frederick Case, 2:2046–50. Chicago: Illinois University Press, 2013.

Yorke, Gosnell L., and Peter Renju, eds. *Bible Translation and African Languages.* Nairobi: Acton, 2004.

Young, Robert. *White Mythologies.* New York: Routledge, 2004.

CPSIA information can be obtained
at www.ICGtesting.com
Printed in the USA
LVHW012044140319
610723LV00007B/35

9 781532 641824